Founded in 1942 in Erie, Pennsylvania by Orange F. Merwin and his son, Robert, Eriez Magnetics has developed products, systems and procedures from which other small and medium-sized companies can learn. And the lessons are more far-reaching than simply operations and helpful hints. The focus of the Eriez story is its corporate Golden Rule. It proves that good people can finish first!

In this book, companies will gain important insights into the establishment of an outside board of directors, venturing into foreign markets, leveraging advertising and communications to dominate markets, developing a system for nearly 90% on-time delivery, introducing new technology through an active R&D effort, and more. By reading this book, Eriez' customers will understand their supplier better. But even more significantly, virtually every Eriez technology appears in easy-to-read, easy-to-understand terms. You'll read about superconducting magnetic separation systems, metal detection, vibratory feeders, magnets, screen separators, rare earth plates/grates/traps and eddy current separators, among others. Eriez holds a special place in separation technology since it is the only magnet company offering five major types of separation: eddy current, electromagnetic, permanent magnetic, electrostatic and screen separation.

Business students will discover that Eriez is a company worth studying. They'll find the book replete with examples and case studies that provide practical guidance for the companies that make this nation hum — small companies with fewer than 500 employees.

To increase the technical knowledge of the reader, Eriez has selected exclusive magnetic tables, data, and general information to make up the valuable appendix.

Eriez Magnetics' Golden Rule provides for the best possible treatment of customers, employees, suppliers, shareholders and the community. This book treats the reader to a story of success, technology and friendship that is a special blend for a special company. It's good reading. A case study. A technology overview. All in one.

ERIEZ MAGNETICS
FROM PIONEER
TO WORLD LEADER

A HISTORY OF THE COMPANY

Michael J. McQuillen, PhD.

Professor of History, Mercyhurst College

CONTENTS

INTRODUCTION   1

Chapter I: THE PIONEER YEARS, 1942-1951   3

Chapter II: THE RISE TO WORLD STATUS, 1952-1961   33

Chapter III: STAYING AT THE TOP, 1962-1991   59

APPENDIX   101

INTRODUCTION

This is the story of the Eriez Manufacturing Company, or Eriez Magnetics, as it is better known, a little company that dared to be great. With just over $50 million in sales and barely 500 employees, this small firm is dwarfed by the billion-dollar conglomerates with thousands of workers that normally dominate an industry. Despite its modest size, Eriez set out to climb the hill that led to recognition as the world leader in its field.

Through a commitment to the motivating vision and guiding values provided by the Merwin family, this enterprise began literally in the basement of the family home and grew into an advanced technology company. Today, it is the world's largest manufacturer of magnetic and other types of separation equipment and a major producer of vibratory, conveying and metal detection equipment for processing industries.

Few American companies its size are as diverse in product, market and geography as is Eriez. Almost none is as globally-minded. With extensive export sales to over eighty countries and with manufacturing facilities in eight nations spanning five continents, it is fair to say that the sun never sets on Eriez operations. Wherever and whenever someone needs to separate, purify, concentrate, recover, recycle, move, or precisely feed any type of material, it is safe to assume that Eriez, with over 1,000 types and sizes of process industry equipment, has the products and processes best suited to get the desired results. The finest research and testing facilities in the industry allow Eriez to stay at the forefront of technology and keep one step ahead of the competition with new product development and new applications.

As it passes its 50th anniversary year in 1992, it is fitting to look at the factors behind Eriez' success. Like most companies that rise to a position of world leadership in their field, Eriez has built its position on a solid base of quality products and service, talented management, first-rate advertising and marketing, a top-notch engineering team, and capable, hard-working, loyal people.

In addition, a pioneering spirit, a world-oriented mentality, a refusal to become self-satisfied, and a determination to be the best at what it does have all been hallmarks of the company since its inception. Guided by a Fundamental Principle ingrained in the company by the founding Merwin family, Eriez management has also fashioned a corporate culture that respects, rewards and motivates all employees.

Finally, one of the most important qualities that has marked the history of the company throughout its growth from basement operation to world leader is the pride that the company's people have always taken in a product well-made and a job well-done. This pride that Eriez people take in the products and services they provide is exceeded only by the pride Eriez takes in its employees.

CHAPTER 1

THE PIONEER YEARS
1942-1951

===

"How dull it is to pause, to make an end,
To rust unburnished, not to shine in use,…
Some work of noble note, may yet be done,…
Come my friends,
'Tis not too late to seek a newer world,…
To strive, to seek, to find, and not to yield."
"Ulysses"
—Alfred, Lord Tennyson

In the summer and fall of 1941 a traveling salesman made his rounds through the tri-state area surrounding his Erie, Pennsylvania base. As he talked with grain millers to whom he sold equipment, he once again heard the common complaints that were now only too familiar. Customers told the same stories about damage to their machinery, about livestock becoming ill or dying from their feed, and worst of all, about explosions and fires at the mills. The culprit in all these cases was the same— "tramp iron."

Known as "trash iron" in the South and as "ferrous contamination" to the experts, the tramp iron problem had been the bane of millers for centuries. In countless ways, stray pieces of metal somehow found their way into the grain that farmers brought to the mills for grinding. From tiny bits of wire to nails and bolts, even to horseshoes and hammers, this stray iron would flow down the chute with the grain into the miller's equipment. The larger pieces could seriously damage screens and machinery. The annoyance of having to shut down production was compounded by the expense of making repairs. The smaller pieces made their way into the feedsacks and caused real headaches for farmers. Livestock that ingested the feed often became ill or diseased, and even died. One customer showed him eleven nails and thirteen pieces of baling wire removed from the stomach of a prize cow that recently had died.

More serious than the problem of damaged machinery or contaminated product was the danger of explosion and fire. Grain dust can be highly explosive. A spark caused by stray metal hitting rapidly moving machinery could literally blow a company out of business.

The salesman who, on the eve of the Second World War, listened so patiently and sympathetically to his customers' tales of woe possessed an uncommon name and an even more uncommon spirit. Orange Fowler Merwin, known to all his friends simply as "O.F.", was already nearly seventy years old. Still hard at work on the road because he could not afford to retire, he yet retained the active, inquiring mind and enterprising spirit of his youth. He also still clung to his life-long dream of being his own boss. The story of his life proves in striking fashion that one is never too old to act on a good idea and never too old to pursue one's dream.

O. F. Merwin was born in Braceville, Ohio on December 28, 1871. After graduating from the Normal School in Valparaiso, Indiana, he returned to his small northeastern Ohio hometown to teach school. Like so many of his male counterparts at the time, however, he soon abandoned the classroom for other pursuits. In 1903 he moved to Erie, Pennsylvania and found employment as a bookkeeper for a roofing company at the then respectable salary of $28 a month. Shortly thereafter, he married his childhood sweetheart and former pupil, Louise Regal, and brought her to Erie. A self-admitted advocate of the adage "work for yourself, then you can be your own boss," O.F. soon saw an opportunity to strike off on his own.

After moving into a purchasing position, he became aware of the chronic shortage of metal disks used to hold down roofing paper. Since no one was making these disks on a regular basis, he purchased a few old punch presses and opened the Merwin Manufacturing Company, a sheet metal stamping works at 19th and Holland Streets. The company never prospered as O.F. hoped and during the First World War he gave up control to William Decker. To this day the company still bears the Merwin name.

In the meantime, O.F. tried several other ventures at self-employment. In 1917 he opened the Erie Penn Auto Company, a distributor of Chandler Six automobiles. In the late 1920's and the early 1930's O.F. alternated between working as a manager for the Campbell Coal Company and trying to establish himself as an independent coal broker.

In 1932, the Campbell Company fell victim, like so many businesses, to the Great Depression. O.F. then associated himself with the Fairfield Engineering Company as a sales representative for its line of milling and conveying equipment. Operating out of his office in the Commerce Building, he spent the next decade visiting small feed mills and coal yards in northeastern Ohio, northwestern Pennsylvania, and western New York. His dream of being his own boss seemed forever buried in the economic debris left by the Depression.

By the end of 1941 the country was finally pulling out of its economic plunge and O.F. was on the verge of one final chance at making it on his own. He had been thinking for a long time about his customers' problems with tramp iron. Then one day an idea came to him. While visiting his close friend, Marve Reynolds, in his automobile repair garage at 3rd and State Streets, O.F. accidentally knocked over a bucket of spare auto parts. He scurried about trying to pick up the rolling pieces. He soon looked up, startled, to see his friend using a magnet from an old magneto to round up the scattered pieces. On his way home, fascinated by the ease and speed with which the magnet had swept the floor clean, he made a momentous connection.

O.F. had long been aware that many millers tried to solve their tramp iron problems with magnets. But the electromagnets utilized by the large mills were expensive, cumbersome, difficult to install, and unreliable. The chrome-cobalt horseshoe magnets used by the small mills weren't powerful enough and ultimately lost what magnetic strength they had. Now he remembered an article he just had read about a new magnetic alloy called Alnico.

Dutch and English metallurgists discovered that alloys containing a certain percentage of aluminum, nickel, cobalt and iron (hence the name Alnico) possessed exceptional magnetic properties. Peak magnetic strength was up to 30 times that of cobalt steel and these alloys retained their strength seemingly forever. In the late 1930's the new Alnico magnets were designed into improved radio speakers, motors, and communications equipment.

What if, O.F. thought to himself, some of these new permanent magnets were fashioned into magnetic separators and attached to grain chutes? This could be the solution to the tramp iron problem! He became so excited about his idea that he almost drove through the closed door of his garage. The following day he approached Reynolds with a request. Could he help O.F. construct a plate magnet that would fit on the bottom of a chute and be hinged to swing open for cleaning? O.F. made a rough sketch of his proposed "permanent magnetic separator." Reynolds said he could build it.

Later that night O.F.'s son and daughter-in-law, Bob and Betty, stopped by the house for a visit. They listened attentively as O.F. explained his idea. "All I need," he concluded, "is some money to make one of the things." Betty noted that she had saved some money from her earnings as a schoolteacher and would be happy to make it available. The next day she brought over a check for $351. Betty's faith was impressive since O.F.'s knowledge of magnets extended only to the fact that they attracted iron. Marve Reynolds, moreover, was no engineer but only a mechanic of the "if I can get my hands on it, I can figure out how it works" school.

Armed with his daughter-in-law's venture capital and his friend's mechanical ability, O.F. set out to make his idea a reality. After learning that the General Electric Company had secured a royalty agreement from the Phillips Company of Eindhoven, Holland to produce Alnico castings in North America, he bought a few castings along with some steel, brass, and

O.F. Merwin displays an early model of the permanent magnetic plate separator he developed with Marve Reynolds.

a used hacksaw. Soon, in the basement of the Merwin residence at 939 West 7th Street a prototype non-electric magnetic plate separator began to take shape. O.F. and Marve quickly learned not to work with already magnetized Alnico when building the separator. The magnets kept grabbing out of their hands the steel pieces with which they were trying to fashion the plate and insulating strips. Magnetizing the Alnico must be the final step.

After a few weeks of trial-and-error tinkering in the evening hours, they at last completed a working model. Two U-shaped Alnico magnets were attached to two steel plates surrounded by brass strips to prevent magnetic forces from leaking to the metal chute.

Early in 1942, O.F. took his demonstrator to a small country mill in nearby Sharon, Pennsylvania. The owner of the Roux Feed Mill was a friend and customer. After attaching the separator to the bottom of the mill's feed chute, O.F. dropped some odd pieces of iron into a bag of grain and emptied it down the chute. The magnet pulled every metal piece from the grain flow. Impressed by the results, the miller agreed to keep the separator in for a trial period.

Following each day's milling, the operator unhinged the plate and scraped off the day's harvest of tramp iron. In a week he collected two handfuls of nails, wires, nuts, and bolts, as well as a jackknife he'd lost a month before. He proudly showed his customers all the tramp iron he was keeping out of their feed; he also talked his insurance agent into lowering his premium on his fire insurance policy. When O.F. returned, the operator not only asked to keep the demonstrator, but ordered two additional units as well.

With this first sale of $150 in April, 1942, O.F. recouped nearly half of Betty's investment. At an age when most men have already been in retirement for several years, O.F. was about to set himself up in business once again. Only this time he would remain his own boss for good.

With the success of his product demonstrated, O.F. recognized he would need help to produce and market his magnetic separators. He asked his son if he would be interested in joining him in a general partnership. Seeing the potential opportunities in the new venture, Bob quickly agreed. In December of the following year, they officially brought their wives, Louise and Betty, into the family partnership. None of them could have truly foreseen what was to follow.

First, the new company needed a name. Their first two choices—the Merwin Manufacturing Company and the Erie Manufacturing Company— were already claimed. They eventually settled on O.F.'s suggestion of the

Eriez Manufacturing Company, after the original Indian tribe from which both the city and the adjacent lake derived their name. They selected "Chief Eriez", an Indian head with a warbonnet, as the company's trademark.

O.F. set about organizing the production process and planning a sales campaign. His Commerce Building office became the company's headquarters. Word of mouth about this remarkably effective and inexpensive little safeguard spread around the region and led to a number of unsolicited orders; but most of the initial year's sales came from the door to door approach. O.F. called on scores of mills, farms, co-ops and grain elevators in the area. When he met with resistance or skepticism, he turned to a favorite proposal. He offered to install a demonstrator to the bottom of a grain chute or hammermill feed table and return in a couple of days. The miller would then either buy the unit or O.F. would pour what had been collected back down the chute into the hammermill. It proved an effective tactic as no magnets were returned.

To reach markets outside the region the company mounted an extensive direct mail campaign. A stream of letters and brochures poured out to potential customers around the country. By the end of 1942 the first advertisements, designed by Bob, appeared in various trade journals. Eriez also sent numerous letters to salesmen, especially those who handled milling accounts, inviting them to represent Eriez in the field. Bob made calls on manufacturers of hammermills urging them to install Eriez magnetic separators on the feed tables of their machines.

The early sales approach was effective. The literature showed how customers could order a fixed or hinged separator for either a wood or steel chute. All were made to order, in widths ranging in size from 4" to 36" and in cost from $35 to $270. Despite the description of its magnetism as permanent, each magnetic separator came "unconditionally guaranteed for ten years." This may have been out of fear the customer would not believe Eriez magnetic strength would last. By 1947 Alnico's reputation was sufficiently established for Eriez to extend a "lifetime strength guarantee."

To fill the orders generated by this diverse and extensive marketing campaign, O.F. relied on a "cottage industry" style operation. The Merwin home at 939 West 7th Street, which the family had lived in since 1912, became the painting and shipping site of the company.

Obtaining government permission to purchase Alnico magnets proved

The Merwin Residence at 939 W. 7th Street - The birthplace of Eriez Magnetics.

to be one of the company's first problems. During the Second World War many items labelled "critical", such as nickel and cobalt, could only be procured with War Production Board (WPB) approval. Here, Bob's experience first as a newspaperman and later as Priorities Director for Parker White Metal Company proved invaluable. He made several trips to Washington and produced a booklet with names of well-known companies that had purchased Eriez separators coupled with an explanation of why Eriez magnets were so critical to their operations. The severe shortage of copper wire, which significantly curtailed the production of electromagnets, strengthened the company's case. Eventually, Bob succeeded in earning Eriez products a WPB rating of "essentiality." From then on the company had no trouble getting supplies and its customers had no difficulty in gaining approval for purchases.

With the flow of materials assured, O.F. engaged three more "basement" subcontractors to join Marve Reynolds in cutting, sawing and drilling parts into finished magnetic separators. Completed units were then taken to the Briggs-Hagenlocher garage to be energized on their small electrocharger. When a number of the separators were finished, Bob, Betty and their friends dropped by to help clean, paint and pack them.

Within a year, mounting sales required an expansion. Five garage or cellar assembly "plants" emerged. Finishing work continued to be done in the evenings in the Merwin basement. On most evenings a team of four to seven women cleaned filings from the magnets, puttied any cracks, then shellacked and painted them. A "Chief Eriez" trademark decal and metal Eriez nametag were applied. The final steps involved packing the separators and delivering them to Railway Express for shipping. Fortunately, all the people working in the 5'10" high Merwin cellar were 5'8" or shorter.

O.F. now concentrated on purchasing and production, while Bob focused on sales. To help out in the Commerce Building office, O.F. hired Beth Driscoll. Beth, who retired in 1973 after 30 years of service as Eriez' chief order clerk, once described those early days in the office: "We had one typewriter and a couple of desks. Mr. Merwin had one desk and I had the other. We had no adding machine or postage meter. We sent out our standard direct mail pieces and processed orders by hand." There was no shortage, however, of energy and enthusiasm.

To assist with the sprawling production operation, in 1944 the company hired its first full-time male employee, Conrad "Cuni" Johannesen. He had actually started the year before as a part-time painter in the Merwin basement. Over the next two years Cuni was an invaluable handyman, deliveryman, and night foreman.

By the end of 1944 the signs of the company's success were indisputable. Sales topped $113,000 compared to $8,333 in 1942. Where the company produced 112 separators in its first year, it shipped 3,000 in 1944. When a firm in Rhode Island purchased a unit, Eriez magnets had been sold in every state in the Union, as well as in Canada and Mexico. A nationwide network of sales representatives was beginning to appear.

Testimonial letters praising the company's product came pouring in. The owner of one of the West Coast's biggest processing companies wrote: "The magnets are astonishing to say the least. I really had no idea that such power could be exerted by a permanent magnet and everyone who comes in says the same thing." A mill foreman in Minnesota wrote: "This has been one of the most trouble-free separators we have ever used;...nothing has ever passed it that has done any harm at all to our machine." From a feed mill in Florida came this claim: "Prior to installing your magnet we were having a great many complaints from our customers regarding tramp iron and metal, but since installing it we have not had one single complaint." An insurance company, Factory Mutual, reduced mill insurance rates for companies that installed Eriez magnets.

While the bulk of the company's sales continued to be made to the milling industry, an impressive array of customers began to appear in a wide variety of other markets. Among the "big name" companies already using Eriez separators by this time were Dow and DuPont in the chemical industry;

Sherwin Williams and Glidden in the paint industry; Goodyear and Firestone in the rubber industry; and General Mills, Heinz, and Campbell Soup in the food processing industry. It was this glimmer of the potential uses for Eriez' products in a broad range of fields, coupled with a fateful trip taken the following year by Bob and Betty Merwin, that brought the company in 1945 to one of the important turning points in its history.

In the summer before V-J Day, the younger Merwins decided to take a sales trip to the southeastern part of Pennsylvania. During the two-week trip to Philadelphia and back they visited a dozen different manufacturers. "We found to our surprise," Bob later recalled, "that not only feed and flour mills had tramp iron problems. Almost every industry had some sort of ferrous contamination headache. Why, there were new customers around every corner! Our job was simply to find them and show them how we could solve their problems."

Find them they did. A miller connected with the Bachman Chocolate Factory in Elizabethtown, Pa., for example, took Bob and Betty to meet the owner. The plant was experiencing fires breaking out in mills that pulverized cocoa beans. Bob showed him that where there is fire, there is need for a magnet. The chocolate maker immediately ordered eight small separators. The next stop was at the Hershey Chocolate Company where the first of scores of Eriez magnets was ordered. Upon stopping at a mattress factory, they found the owner complaining of everything from bottle caps to baling wire in the second-hand cotton he bought. He had never thought of using magnets, but admitted they sounded like a good way of getting the junk out.

And so it went. Of the twelve factories visited, ten placed orders. "When Mrs. Merwin and I returned from that trip," Bob noted years later, "we had earned $2,500 in commissions from the orders. A princely sum! Better than the money, however, was our discovery that we had a product with a future. Most important, my father, now in his early 70's, knew that both success and security had come to him. His idea was sound; the market was out there; the rest was up to us."

A few weeks later, Robert discussed the future of the company with O.F. He described the tremendous potential that existed, especially if Eriez could develop additional products to meet the special needs of different industries. O.F. was quite content producing just the plate-type magnetic separators. However, if Eriez was to branch into new fields and develop new products, that was up to his son. Whatever he wanted to do was fine with O.F. "The decision was to diversify," as Bob put it. A couple of years later, O.F. would tell a news reporter that Eriez' movement into scores of different industries was "due to the vision of his son." As "Cuni" Johannesen put it: "Bob Merwin had the foresight to see what the company could become."

Robert Freeman Merwin was born in Erie on December 21, 1913. In 1932 he entered Hiram College in Ohio, where he majored in economics and served as editor of the college paper. In his freshman year he met a bright and attractive young History/English major from Cleveland by the name of Betty MacKay. A close friendship developed.

After their graduation in 1936 Betty went to teach in a Cleveland high school while Robert went to work for a newspaper in Ravenna, Ohio. His father had wanted him to become a salesman, but Bob's true love was journalism. After a year as County Editor for the Ravenna Record, he returned to Erie to take a job with the Dispatch-Herald. He found the next three years as an editorial and general reporter both enjoyable and educational but financially unrewarding. This became more important after he and Betty MacKay married in June, 1940. In 1942 he accepted Robert Parker's offer to join the Parker White Metal Company as Priorities Director and Assistant Purchasing Agent.

Though he had left his job at Parker White in 1943 to work full-time for the new partnership, it was only after that 1945 downstate trip that Bob Merwin recognized the true potential of the company. With his father's blessing and support, he now set out to realize that potential. He knew what needed to be done. Larger facilities for the company had to be found. New products had to be developed and a broader and more sophisticated market-

The Founding Family, (circa 1943): Louise R., Betty M., Orange F., and Robert F. Merwin.

ing approach needed to be adopted. A larger and more diverse sales network had to be built, an engineering department established, and experienced manufacturing and marketing personnel recruited. It was a bold plan; and on its success depended the future of the company.

The Eriez Manufacturing Company was officially incorporated on October 31, 1946 with an initial capitalization of $64,000. The 640 shares (at $100 par value each) were distributed among the four family members. O.F. Merwin was named president; R. F. Merwin, vice-president; Betty, secretary; and Louise, treasurer of the new corporation.

In June, 1945 the Merwins purchased manufacturing and engineering facilities at 912 West 12th Street and expanded the Commerce Building office. The 8,000 square foot production shop enabled the company to centralize production and eliminate the part-time basement operations. Built into the new plant was Eriez' first magnetic separation testing facility.

The enlarged plant made it possible to tackle new industry problems. Early in 1945, an engineer with the Factory Insurance Association approached Eriez to help reduce the disturbing level of fire losses in textile mills. The engineer, Scott Goodwin, estimated that about 10% of the fires in these mills resulted from stray iron reaching machinery. Working together with Bob Merwin, they determined that a plate-type separator suspended over the discharge end of the spiked-apron feeders in the mills would remove all the stray iron. After an experimental installation proved the validity of this approach, the first separator for the textile industry was sold to a company in New Bedford, Massachusetts. This spiked-apron separator proved especially popular among bedding manufacturers and cotton mill processors.

A short while later Eriez developed yet another solution to the industry's fire-hazard problem—the magnetic hump. Most cotton mills relied on pneumatic feed lines to bring the cotton into opening and carding rooms. To reduce the risk of fire and machinery damage from metal pieces in the cotton, Bob designed and patented a unique "hump" to be inserted in these air lines. The hump, with its two 45-degree angles, disrupted the material flow and trapped the iron against one of two strategically placed plate magnets. So effective were the spiked-apron and hump separators that in 1947 the textile industry replaced milling as Eriez' single largest market. In the process, the textile industry reduced tramp iron fires virtually to zero. Also, when installed in a vertical flow, the Eriez magnetic hump provided another ideal solution to the ferrous contamination problem.

The addition of larger and stronger permanent magnets enabled the company to move into yet more fields. In 1946 Eriez introduced the

"Jumbo", which was 25% stronger than the original "Standard" plate magnet. The following year it unveiled the "Giant", with 50% more "pulling power." Their greater strength made it possible to handle material flows of greater depth and speed than ever before. The "Giant" played a major role in opening the field of heavy industry to permanent magnetic separation. Its effective range of 4-5" (compared to 1-2" for the "Standard") meant that materials such as coal, rock products and slag could now be cleansed of unwanted iron. Eriez early on also developed a magnetic trap to purify liquids and slurries in pipelines of ferrous particles.

One of the major limitations to all of Eriez permanent separators was the need for employees to manually clean iron contamination from the face of the magnets. With the introduction of the non-electric magnetic pulley in

O.F. Merwin stands behind a permanent magnetic pulley, first developed in 1946.

1946 Eriez took the first of what would become several steps towards the development of a self-cleaning, non-electric magnetic separator.

The Eriez pulley resulted from a challenge presented to the company by the B.F. Goodrich Company. In 1945 an Eriez representative visited the superintendent of Goodrich's Reclaiming Division in Akron, Ohio to demonstrate the plate magnetic separator. He was taken to the processing unit where electrically powered magnetic head pulleys removed bead wire from shredded rubber moving along ten conveyor lines. Under nearly continuous operating conditions, the electromagnetic pulleys tended to burn out after only nine months of use. "Let me make a suggestion," said the plant manager. "If you can design and build a permanent magnetic pulley that removes the wire as well as these electros, we'll buy them rather than have the electros repaired."

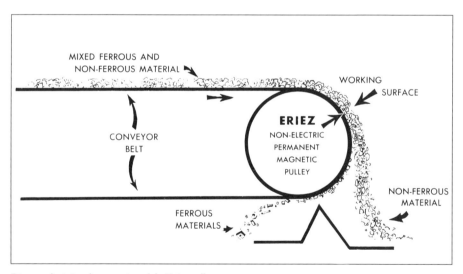

Diagram depicting the operation of the Eriez pulley.

Bob Merwin decided to accept the challenge. He located two consulting engineers in Akron, W. C. Pothoff and his assistant, Ronnie Hoff, who agreed to work on the project. They had no design experience in the area of permanent magnetic separation (neither did anyone else at that time), but felt that the job could be done. Only thirteen months later, after one false start and many modifications, Eriez delivered the first Alnico-powered, self-cleaning permanent magnetic pulley. As the material flow reached this new pulley, its powerful magnetic field held any tramp iron to the belt while the non-ferrous material fell freely off the conveyor. The unwanted iron was discharged behind a divider at a point where the belt left contact with the pulley's magnetic field. Delighted with the pulley's performance, Goodrich kept its word and eventually replaced all of its electromagnetic pulleys with Eriez models.

Eriez permanent pulleys soon found widespread application in a host of situations where processors and producers used conveyor belts to move materials. Eriez quickly developed another important self-cleaning magnet not requiring a conveyor belt. The permanent magnetic drum consisted of a semi-circular stationary magnet placed inside a nonmagnetic revolving shell. Nonferrous material falling on top of the shell fell off at the three o'clock position. Ferrous material, attracted by the stationary magnet, would cling to the shell surface until it passed the magnetic field and dropped off after passing a material divider plate located at the six o'clock posi-
tion.

To reach a wider range of customers for the company's new or improved products, Bob Merwin launched an intensive advertising campaign. In 1945 he drafted Eriez' first full-page, two-color ads and placed them in a variety of trade journals. Over

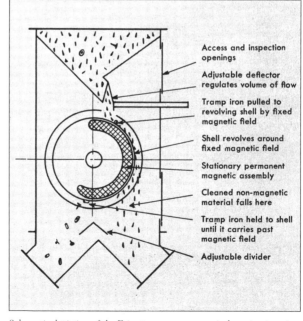

Access and inspection openings

Adjustable deflector regulates volume of flow

Tramp iron pulled to revolving shell by fixed magnetic field

Shell revolves around fixed magnetic field

Stationary permanent magnetic assembly

Cleaned non-magnetic material falls here

Tramp iron held to shell until it carries past magnetic field

Adjustable divider

Schematic depiction of the Eriez permanent magnetic drum in operation.

the next couple of years such ads provided case studies of effective installations, stressed the endorsement of Eriez magnets by the Mill Mutual, Factory
Mutual, and Factory Insurance associations, and touted the advantages of
permanent over electromagnetic separators. To provide first-hand experience with Eriez separators company sales representatives carried demonstrator magnets on their calls. And O.F., Robert, and Betty Merwin all enjoyed
the crowds of potential customers attracted to Eriez displays at trade shows
around the country.

As important as ads in journals and appearances at trade shows were,
Robert knew that a far-flung and knowledgeable sales force was even more
vital to the company's growth. The initial group of agents, mostly with
milling backgrounds, knew little about the textile, food, chemical or other
industries. He thus recruited additional representatives with experience in
general industry. He convinced a number of outstanding salesmen to
represent Eriez through their offices in New York City, Philadelphia,
Cleveland, Pittsburgh, Detroit, Chicago, Atlanta, St. Louis and Kansas
City. They not only aggressively sought out orders, but also used their
experience and ingenuity to find surprising new uses for Eriez separators.

To keep its representatives abreast of the many new products and their
myriad applications, Eriez began in 1945 to publish a series of industrial sales
bulletins. Two years later the company organized its first Sales Conference
in Erie. Held annually until 1951 and every other year thereafter, these
conferences provided valuable opportunities for Eriez' men in the field to get
to know the company's people and products better.

Between 1945 and 1947, new facilities, an expanded product line, a
broader advertising campaign and an extensive sales force all played significant roles in helping the company achieve Bob and Betty Merwin's goal of
moving Eriez beyond the stage of a make-shift operation producing magnets
for just the grain industry. The most important move made in this period to
ensure the company's continued growth was the addition of a core of vital
new personnel.

Bob's experience in developing the magnetic pulley and drum and in developing new magnetic assemblies for the textile industry convinced him that Eriez' real strength lay not so much in its products as in its problem-solving capability. He realized that once the initial "simple and easy" installations were exhausted, future sales would hinge on meeting the challenges posed by each customer's unique separation problem. As these problems became more technical and complex, Eriez would need much greater expertise than it then possessed. Fortunately, especially in production, engineering, and research and development, Bob recruited several key figures whose contributions to Eriez would continue for years, even decades, to come.

The need for a skilled mechanic and machinist was met when Dick Dickey, who learned his trade at Erie Forge, became the company's third full-

Some of the key personnel on the early Eriez team: seated (left to right): George Wellmon, Robert Merwin, O.F. Merwin, Maggie Flynn; standing (left to right): Ronnie Hoff, Cuni Johannesen, Al Amidon, Dick Roosevelt, Harry March.

time employee in December, 1945. Dickey became the Shop Foreman when
the West 12th Street plant opened. In January, 1946, O.F. Merwin told a
young former procurement officer in the Air Force: "Stick around and do
what you can. Some day we're going to set up a Purchasing Department."
G. A. (Al) Amidon did. Six months later he was named head of Shipping
and Receiving at the new plant and the following year appointed
Purchasing Agent. A month after hiring Amidon, Eriez recruited R. A.
(Dick) Roosevelt, an Erie General Electric advertising executive, to help
build the Eriez advertising department. Three years later he assumed the
crucial position of Sales Manager. His services proved invaluable in both
positions.

One of the most important additions to the Eriez staff in this period was
Ronnie C. Hoff. Having learned about the company through his work on the
magnetic pulley, Hoff agreed to join Eriez in mid-1947 as Engineering and
Plant Manager. Along with years as an independent consultant, he brought
fifteen years experience with the Goodyear Aircraft Corporation to his new
position. In 1947 Emerson Tenpas joined the growing Eriez engineering
staff. "Em", who had just recently completed his mechanical engineering
degree at the University of Pittsburgh, was put in charge of the Test
Laboratory. This initial lab consisted of one balance scale, one chute with
a plate magnet in it, a magnetic pulley and a drum. Under the direction of
Tenpas and his successors, Eriez would build one of the finest magnetic
testing facilities in the world. Walt Lukowski, hired in March, 1947 as a
design engineer, also provided valuable engineering services to the company.

Playing a major part in Eriez early growth was Maggie Flynn, who had
two decades of business office experience in New York City. Upon returning
to Erie she was immediately recruited as Eriez office manager. Loving the job
with a growing new company needing help, she worked tirelessly to get Eriez
paperwork systems organized.

With the assistance of these and other key personnel, Eriez began to build a reputation for quality engineering, quick delivery and efficient service that was to become its most important asset. Reflecting this reputation, Eriez' sales reached the million dollar level in 1947. The company's customer list read like a "Who's Who" of American business. Only two short years after committing themselves to a program of growth and diversification, the Merwins could hardly keep track of the startling variety of uses for Eriez products.

The U.S. Treasury used an Eriez separator to remove from circulation the steel pennies issued during the war to conserve copper. An Ohio chemical plant turned to Eriez to keep itself from literally being run out of town. With the plant averaging five explosions a week, the city government asked the manufacturer to leave because of the danger and the staggering cost to its fire department of responding to so many calls. The firm asked Eriez to install several of its separators. The explosions stopped and the company stayed. Recording companies used Eriez magnets to remove from vinyl compounds the iron contaminants that caused damage to stamper machines and the needles of record players.

Applications in the food processing industry, which emerged by 1947 as the second leading industrial group using Eriez products, seemed endless. Gerber, Beechnut and others used magnetic separators to keep their baby food pure. Chocolate manufacturers used them to keep their candy free of impurities. Canneries of all kinds used them to eliminate such problems as fish tags in tuna and hairpins in vegetables. Confectioners, bakeries, soup companies and cereal makers likewise sought to protect machines and products with Eriez magnets. So did brewers, distillers, wineries, coffee processors, fruit juice plants and soft drink bottlers.

In heavy and general industry, mines, foundries, rock product companies, paper mills, metal-working firms, refuse plants and utilities employed magnetic separators to protect their pulverizers, crushers, grinders, chippers, stokers, boilers and other machines. Plastics producers, cigarette makers, drug companies, glass works and potteries also installed Eriez magnets.

O.F. and Bob Merwin meet in Commerce Building Office in 1948 to discuss expanding the Eriez product line.

Overall satisfaction with the results could be seen in the mounting number of repeat orders from many companies. Eriez also received some rather unusual requests during this time that it declined to fill, including magnets to control pinball machines.

Though an impressive array of uses for its products had been discovered and though sales had soared to the million dollar mark after only five years, Eriez was not without its problems. Some of the difficulties it faced were more amusing than serious; but others threatened the company's health and even its very existence.

On the humorous side, Eriez sales representatives learned there could be peculiar hazards to their trade of peddling magnets. Several such hazards were recounted in an excellent article on Eriez published by the Saturday Evening Post in 1953. One salesman boarded a plane from Erie to Cleveland. Following the proper compass direction, the pilot found himself heading across the lake to Canada instead of along the shore to Cleveland. He abruptly altered course and flew the rest of the way by sight. As the salesman left the plane he overheard the pilot shout to the service crew, "Yank out that compass. The thing's ninety degrees off." The passenger paused for a moment, then approached the crew cabin. "I think this is what threw off your compass," he said. He showed the pilot a permanent magnet inside his briefcase. Thereafter, Eriez people marked their baggage "Place in rear of plane." Complaints also came from railroad and trucking companies. Eriez crates would occasionally arrive plastered with scraps of iron, tools, and even other packages that had iron in them.

Another salesman found that traveling with magnets could even be troublesome on elevators. On the way to his hotel floor, the salesman noticed a woman in front of him moving steadily backward as several passengers entered the elevator. Suddenly, his briefcase swung up and swatted her from behind. It seems the metal stays in her corset were simply too attractive for the magnet in his briefcase. He quickly slipped off at the next floor. Then there was the salesman who carried a magnet through an office on his way to see the plant engineer. As he passed a secretary, she let out a yell and grabbed her hair. Inside the engineer's office he found his magnet covered with hairpins. Such incidents taught the company to use "keeper bars" to tame its magnets when not in use. These iron bars were placed across the poles to close the magnetic circuit and reduce the field of attraction.

There were also a few customer complaints. One person, impressed by the company's claims about the strength of Alnico magnets, bought a Standard casting and then returned it because it would not attract objects 300 feet away! A foundry in Pittsburgh called to complain that its "permanent" magnetic separators were weakening. Impossible, thought Bob Merwin, but still sent an Eriez engineer to check things out. He found the separators were weakening—because someone had removed several of the magnet castings. The culprit turned out to be an employee who used them to develop an amazing skill with pinball machines.

On the more serious side, the company faced concerns about "market saturation." Ever since its inception Eriez had heard claims that it would be a short-lived company. After an initial flurry of sales, many predicted, it would soon be out of customers and out of business. After all, the company contained the seeds of its own destruction. Since its products used "permanent" magnets, replacement orders would be non-existent. New markets might be found for a time, but ultimately orders would dry up. The emergence of strong competition would hasten this day.

And it was not long before such competition did emerge. For a few years Eriez had the permanent magnetic market to itself; its only real competitors in the separation field were the four electromagnetic separator manufacturers in existence in 1942. But Eriez' products were relatively simple and easy to copy. By 1948 over thirty firms had begun manufacturing permanent magnetic separators. Two of them were started by former Eriez representatives. Alnico producers encouraged this growth in a drive to sell more of their product.

In addition, the two largest electromagnetic manufacturers adopted the "if you can't beat them, then join them" philosophy. By the late 1940's they were producing and aggressively marketing their own permanent magnetic equipment. One of them had earlier taken out ads asserting that there was no such thing as a permanent magnet and claimed Eriez magnets would lose their strength. Though he did not relish the competition, O.F. felt a sense of gratification when that company began producing permanent magnetic products of its own.

Faced with this growing competition, Eriez sales leveled off in 1948 and declined by 20% the following year. As the critics prepared to say "I told you so," the Merwins responded to the challenge. They incorporated the new Alnico $\underline{V}$ alloy, with virtually double the magnetic field strength of the earlier Alnicos, into their products. Eriez engineers redesigned the pulleys and drums, making them magnetically stronger and more rugged. They added the "Micro-magnetic Separator" in 1950 for removing extremely fine contaminants from powders and other thin material flows. They also introduced a line of magnets for sweeping roads, floors, driveways and yards and for retrieving parts from tanks and vats.

In another move to expand its product line, Eriez began selling RCA Metal Detectors in 1948 and became the sole national distributor for the detectors two years later. Sales proved disappointing, however, and Eriez soon abandoned the line (though, as we shall see, the company would reenter this field in later years.) Far more successful and of much greater significance than this brief flirtation with metal detectors was the company's entrance into the field of magnetic conveying equipment. In 1949 Eriez installed its first magnetic Pipe Rolls at Republic Steel. Within a year the company was offering an array of magnetic rolls, sheet fanners, and other equipment to help move and control steel and steel parts. Eriez soon became an important supplier of automation equipment to the steel and metalworking industries.

To help market its revamped product line the company launched a new advertising campaign. Several ads stressed survey results that showed Eriez the clear first choice of manufacturers asked to rate magnetic separators. Seeking to capitalize on the fascination with things "atomic" at the time and to stress the revolutionary strength of the new line of Alnico $\underline{V}$ plate separators, ads announced the arrival of "ATOMagnets" in 1950 and described them as coming in three strengths: "extra power", "ultra power", and "super power." The following year a set of catchy, cartoon-style ads appeared featuring "Chief Eriez" battling "Mr. Tramp Iron." The Chief was dropped, however, as the company's trademark in 1950 after a survey revealed that scores of companies used an Indian head trademark. The company adopted as its new symbol the distinctive horseshoe magnet above the word "Eriez" connected by flux lines.

Bob and Betty Merwin also recognized the potential of foreign markets. Eriez had received unsolicited orders from Canada and Mexico as early as

Bob and Betty Merwin prepare to depart on one of their many overseas flights to build Eriez' international markets.

1944 and from Latin America since 1946. If such business dropped in their laps with no sales effort whatsoever, the Merwins wondered, what could they achieve with a concerted campaign to generate overseas orders? Since the company lacked any knowledge of such matters as currency exchange rates, letters of credit, customs regulations, import-export licenses and the like, it first relied on an export agency to solicit additional foreign clients.

Soon, however, the Merwins realized that if they had learned and developed their domestic business from scratch, why couldn't they do likewise in international trade? In 1948 they set up an Export Sales Department within the company. This department recruited international sales representatives, took out ads in foreign journals, and established direct contact with customers outside the country. It also provided much better technical assistance and service than any outside agency could.

Bob and Betty took a direct role in cultivating the Latin American market, which was seen as potentially the most lucrative. In 1948 they flew to Brazil, Argentina, Uruguay and Cuba to get a firsthand look at these countries and to line up distributors for Eriez products. As a result of this trip and the efforts of the new Export Sales Department, sales in the region, especially in Brazil, climbed rapidly. By 1950 Eriez had made the transformation from a casual exporter to an aggressive overseas marketer.

Beyond the search for broader markets and new or improved products, Eriez met the challenge presented by its competitors in another important way. From the shop to the accounting office the company brought in several dynamic and capable individuals to further strengthen the Eriez team. Most of these new staff additions brought with them extensive experience that the company immediately put to good use. When combined with the personnel already recruited, this new talent gave the Eriez Manufacturing Company an unmatched ability to provide quality products and service in the areas of magnetic separation and conveying.

One of the important new faces at Eriez was Earl C. Miller, who brought with him more than sixteen years of experience, the last nine of which were in production management. Originally hired as a technical correspondent, Miller's management skills well qualified him for his appointments in 1949 as General Office Manager and in 1951 as Executive Assistant. As Export Sales Manager after 1950 he also played a major part in developing Eriez' foreign markets.

In 1950 the company selected Arlo Israelson as Chief Engineer. With more than seventeen years experience in design engineering and production management in New York, Pennsylvania and California, Israelson was made responsible for all engineering operations and for creating a research and development department. Also, in 1950, James K. Brydon, Jr., came to Eriez to serve as the company's Chief Accountant. A graduate of Ohio University, Jim Brydon had served for ten years as the Chief Cost Accountant for Burke Electric Company in Erie. Brydon's skills would ultimately lead him to be named Vice-President and Treasurer of the company. Another member of Eriez' class of 1950 was Carmen Italia. Employed at first as a boxmaker and truck driver, "Carm" admits to being hired as much for his ballplaying as his carpentry skills (fortunately, he did not compete for Bob Merwin's outfield position). Resourceful and hard-working, Italia rose to shipping clerk and then traffic manager. In those roles he helped build Eriez' enviable reputation for "on time" deliveries.

Around this time, at a plant where Eriez engineers had just completed

General Manager Earl Miller and Sales Manager Dick Roosevelt meeting with O.F. Merwin in 1950.

a successful test run of a newly installed magnetic system, the impressed production superintendent turned to them and asked: "Tell me, how does it happen you people can solve this problem when other magnetic separator manufacturers have failed for the past twenty years?" The answer was simple. No one else had the design, engineering, testing, production, and service personnel that the Merwins had assembled at Eriez Manufacturing Company. Their talent, experience and dedication enabled the company to develop custom-tailored answers to manufacturers' tramp iron problems. Together with the quality of its products, this ability brought Eriez very close to the realization of Robert Merwin's dream that whenever a company faced a separation problem, its first thought would be to come to Eriez for the solution.

All of these measures—the product improvements, the marketing campaigns and the personnel additions—helped Eriez rebound quickly from its disappointing decline in 1949. The following year sales returned to the million dollar level and in 1951 topped $1.3 million.

As the company came to the end of its tenth year of operation, O.F., Robert and Betty Merwin must have noted the contrast between the Eriez of 1951 and the cellar operation from which it had all started. The initial $351 investment had been turned into a company whose net worth exceeded $335,000. The first year's total sales of a little over $8,300 had swollen to well over one million dollars ten years later. The product line had grown from a single plate separator to some thirty-five diverse items. Operations that began in a 500 square foot basement were now conducted in 12,000 square feet of plant space owned by the company and 2,200 square feet of office space rented by it. From not a single full-time employee (even O.F. worked part-time at first) Eriez had expanded to a work force of forty-eight employees. From a solitary salesman (O.F.) making the rounds to local millers had emerged a sales organization with 65 major sales offices in the United States and 37 other countries. The first year closed with 112 separators sold; in 1951 Eriez sold its 50,000th unit to its 20,000th customer;

and these customers could be found in 52 different countries. In short, the Eriez Manufacturing Company in 1951 was the world's largest producer of permanent magnetic separating and conveying equipment. And while that statement also could have been made in 1942, it obviously meant much more a decade later.

CHAPTER 2

THE RISE TO WORLD STATUS
1952-1961

"The great use of life is to spend it
for something which outlasts it."
—William James

In its first decade of existence the Eriez Manufacturing Company had established itself as a pioneer in permanent magnetic technology and the application of that technology to the solution of manufacturers' separation problems. During its second decade Eriez emerged as the world's largest producer of magnetic equipment for the processing industries. It also became the recognized world authority in the fields of materials separation, minerals concentration, and the controlled movement of materials by magnetic and vibratory forces. The story behind that transformation from pioneer to world leader is the focus of this chapter.

Eriez opened the second decade of its corporate life by moving into new quarters. In December, 1951 the Merwins purchased the Northern Equipment Company plant on Grove Drive near the western outskirts of the city of Erie. Over the eleven years that Eriez remained headquartered here, sales quadrupled (from $1 million to $4 million) and the work force tripled (from 50 to 150 employees), necessitating yet another move to more spacious surroundings. In those same years the company made significant improvements in and additions to its original permanent magnetic separation equipment. At the same time, it developed an impressive line of conveying equipment for controlling and moving materials by magnetic and mechanical forces. In a bold move to expand its role in the materials handling field, it introduced a patented line of electromagnetic vibratory feeders and bin vibrators. Toward the end of this period, Eriez also entered the heavy duty electromagnetic equipment field by acquiring a leading producer of such equipment. Finally, Eriez took several steps towards expanding its operations overseas.

The success of these efforts at product development, diversification and overseas expansion can be attributed to the company's continued ability to attract an outstanding array of talented employees. Eriez owed its rise to world prominence to the contribution of the scores of production workers, office staff, sales and marketing personnel, engineers and managers who formed the Eriez team in this period. The key to the company's ability to recruit, retain and motivate these creative and dedicated employees was the management philosophy developed by Bob and Betty Merwin and the corporate culture so carefully nurtured by them. In turn, that philosophy and culture derived from the views and practices of the company's founder, O.F. Merwin. They may, indeed, have been his most important legacy to Eriez.

O.F., unfortunately, did not live to see the dramatic growth of this period. On February 19, 1952, as Eriez was about to enter its second decade, Orange Fowler Merwin died at the age of eighty. He had by then significantly reduced his direct involvement in the company's affairs. Almost to the end, however, he resisted the idea of total retirement. When asked by a reporter in 1948 why, at the age of 76, he had not yet retired, O.F. responded: "That's what they say to men of 70 and if I had listened to them when I was 70, all this wouldn't have happened." Nevertheless, he did begin to spend more time fishing, tending his roses, playing bridge, and vacationing with his wife in Florida. In 1951, with his health declining, he turned over the position of President to his son.

O.F.'s death triggered a flood of fond memories among Eriez employees. Marve Reynolds remembered his "friendly smile," Beth Driscoll his "wholesome sense of humor," and Ronnie Hoff his "sense of value." Cuni

Johannesen recalled how O.F. had treated him "like a son." Curt Shaffer noted how all would miss "Pop" Merwin's visits to the shop and the friendly words he had for everyone. Em Tenpas remembers how quiet O.F. could be on these visits: "He would suddenly just appear next to you." All agreed they would sorely miss the thin little man with the wisp of white hair and the ever present smile.

The local press payed tribute to O.F.'s Horatio Alger-type accomplishments, even if he was considerably older than the typical characters in an Alger story. The Erie Dispatch wrote that he reflected the "pioneering spirit," "rugged individualism," "courage," and "foresight" that "helped make this country great." The paper concluded by noting that if, as William James wrote, "the great use of life is to spend it for something which outlasts it," then O.F. spent his well.

To O.F. the company that represented his "great use of life" was more than just its physical assets. He always cared as much about the character as the profitability of the company he was building. And it was the nature and spirit of the company he shaped more than its plant and products that proved to be O.F.'s greatest gift to Eriez. Like himself, it was a company that embodied the qualities of integrity, foresight, courage, and, above all, concern for others.

A deeply religious man, O.F. firmly believed that a company, like the individual, should operate according to the Golden Rule: "Therefore all things whatsoever ye would that men should do to you, do ye even so to them" (Matthew 7:12). Guided by this conviction, he knew from the start what kind of company he wanted Eriez to be — one that was honest in all its dealings, that cared about its employees, and whose employees cared about others. To create that kind of company O.F. initiated a number of policies and practices that remain an integral part of Eriez today.

"We consider our organization," O.F. once told a reporter, "as one big family, offering help and encouragement when needed." Thus, he always took the time to get to know personally each of the members of his corporate family. He made a point of regularly making the rounds through the plant and offices, never failing, as one veteran worker put it, "to give someone a pat on the back for a job well done." He sought to reward dedication and hard work by always seeking to fill important positions with people from within the company.

Like a family, O.F. believed, Eriez employees should have the opportunity to share good times together. He started first a Christmas Dinner Party and then a summer Family Picnic that remain the social highlights of the company year. In 1947 he encouraged Eriez workers to form their own social organization. In his honor they chose to name it the Orrie-M Club. The club selects its own officers (Cuni Johannesen was elected the first President) and organizes a busy schedule of sporting activities, parties, dances and other events.

Above all, O.F. believed that a company should look out for the well-being of its members and share its good fortune with them. Thus, in 1948 he provided all employees with group accident and medical insurance. Even earlier he had instituted a profit sharing plan whereby 10% of the company's before-tax profits were distributed as a year end bonus to all workers.

Recognizing and rewarding work well done, keeping people informed, providing opportunities to socialize, offering essential benefits, and sharing profits were all characteristics, as the Merwin family saw it, of a company that cared about its employees. They also believed that a company and its people should care about others as well and encouraged civic involvement and charitable activity on the part of Eriez personnel. O.F. set an example himself through his involvement in numerous community activities. He was especially active in the First Christian Church as a member of the Board of Trustees and Sunday School Superintendent.

O.F. encouraged the Orrie-M Club to form a Welfare Committee to consider the needs of people at Eriez and in the community. One of the Committee's oldest efforts at helping the needy is its Christmas Card Fund. Each year just before Christmas a collection is taken up among Eriez workers

This mural, originally commissioned for the lobby of the Grove Drive plant in memory of O.F. Merwin, stresses his commitment to the Golden Rule. It now appears in the Board Room of the company's Asbury Road Headquarters building.

to purchase food baskets and gifts for less fortunate families. This practice originated with a suggestion from O.F. Back in the early days of the company when Eriez magnets were still painted by women working at night, the "paint girls" had a custom of exchanging Christmas cards with each other. One night they engaged in a discussion of the plight of unfortunate families who would not be having a very happy Christmas. They wished they could do something to help. O.F., who had joined in their discussion, recommended that instead of exchanging Christmas cards they donate the money they would have spent on cards and stamps to the Orrie-M Club's Welfare Committee as a Christmas Fund for needy families. They quickly agreed and thereby established one of Eriez' most rewarding traditions.

Upon O.F.'s passing, Bob and Betty Merwin committed themselves to strengthening the culture of integrity and caring that he had cultivated. They first sought to embody his ideals in a formal statement of the company's purpose. Initially adopted in 1952, the Eriez Fundamental Principle clearly enunciated the goals "toward which all effort is expended." The American Management Association was impressed enough with this Principle to include it in its listing of exemplary "Management Creeds and Philoso-

phies." Slightly modified and refined over the years, that Eriez Fundamental
Principle now reads:

> **Using the Golden Rule as a guide…to build a worldwide organi-
> zation that will give OUR CUSTOMERS high quality products
> and services at a favorable price commensurate with good services
> before and after sale; OUR ASSOCIATES the best possible job
> opportunity and work satisfaction; OUR SUPPLIERS every
> opportunity to sell their products and services in an atmosphere
> of courtesy and trust and at prices that will allow them to make
> a fair profit; and OUR STOCKHOLDERS a reasonable continu-
> ing return on their investment. Recognizing our social responsi-
> bility to THE COMMUNITIES in which we operate, we will
> strive to conduct our affairs in such an efficient, capable and
> friendly manner that everyone with whom we come in contact will
> be happy to be associated with us.**

Importantly, as Bob Merwin put it, this statement "is not meaningless
wordage, but the yardstick by which all Eriez plans, policies and decisions
are measured." The enthusiastic commitment of past and present Eriez
personnel to this Principle has been one of the company's most enduring
assets. To foster that commitment the company has stressed that the
cooperation and support of each and every employee is important to the
attainment of its goals. Everyone was seen as a vital part of the Eriez team
and the contribution of each recognized as important to the whole team's
success. All were encouraged to take pride in the company's achievements
and in their own role in bringing them about.

To further associate the success of the individual with the success of the
company, a "promotion from within" policy was adhered to whenever
possible. As Betty Merwin put it, Eriez "has always tried to help people grow
along with the company." To reward those who give particularly outstanding service to the company, Eriez in 1962 instituted an annual Special
Recognition Award renamed in 1988 the Person of the Year Award.

Bob and Betty also took steps to expand the generous benefits package
put together by O.F. Along with a liberal vacation policy and paid lunch
periods, workers gained new insurance coverage and an educational assis-

tance program. The company sought to foster employee savings through the institution of a payroll deduction plan and the establishment of a credit union.

PERSON OF THE YEAR AWARD WINNERS

1962	CONRAD JOHANNESEN	1980	CLARENCE C. MIKOL
1963	ALBERT N. ALLEN	1981	THE DRISTANS
1964	MARY K. McENERY		David A. Walker
1965	JOHN DICKEY		Geraldine A. Baker
1966	NED HIRT		James A. Grumblatt
1967	ATTY. T. E. DOYLE		Josephine M. Jasinski
1968	ALBERT A. STENT		David A. Meyer
1969	ARLO F. ISRAELSON		Dennis L. Salsbury
1970	R. JAMES TORREY	1982	WALTER J. CMIEL
1971	DONALD L. ROSS	1983	DENNIS L. SALSBURY
1972	CARMEN S. ITALIA	1984	GERALD D. ROSE
1973	LOWELL J. HINKSON	1985	DAVID H. McHENRY
1974	EMERSON J. TENPAS	1986	ROSE M. McLAREN
1975	JOHN E. LUTTON	1987	WILLIAM F. DYLEWSKI
1976	JAMES FLOROS	1988	KATHLEEN F. WILLIAMS
1977	FRED L. ADAMS	1989	JOHN L. PALMER
1978	RAYMOND A. COOK	1990	JAMES F. MOORE
1979	CHESTER F. GIERMAK	1991	PAUL M. HOPSECGER

Person of the Year Award Winners.

The success of these and other efforts to make Eriez "an ideal place for employment no matter what the job" is attested to by the fact that Eriez employees have never felt the need for a collective bargaining unit to look after their interests. The only effort ever mounted to form a union at the company went down to resounding defeat in a 1968 NLRB-supervised election. There has never been a work stoppage because of a labor-management grievance in the company's history. The absenteeism rate is impressively low (less than 2% versus an 8% national average). The turnover rate is even lower; the highest number of employees ever to leave in a single year is eight, and five of them were retirees.

Bob and Betty Merwin not only continued and extended O.F.'s "caring" policies towards Eriez personnel, they also encouraged their employees to serve others. As Bob Merwin put it in a speech exhorting his listeners to rise above concern for only their own pleasures and problems:

> To work at the daily routine for no purpose other than to accumulate wealth and the means of satisfying personal needs is to live with inadequate purpose. Unless we feel that we are contributing to someone else's happiness, that the world is the better because we are a part of it, we will not find satisfaction. True joy in life is to be found in being used for a purpose bigger, more important and more lasting than we ourselves are.

The Merwins set an impressive example of living up to this statement for others to follow. Both became active in many civic and charitable organizations. Betty served on boards of over a dozen non-profit bodies, including the International Institute, the YWCA, the American Cancer Society, the Erie Infants Home, Florence Crittendon Services, Gannon and Edinboro Universities, Americans for a Competitive Economic System, the Erie Playhouse, and the Erie Philharmonic. She has been a trustee of Grove City College since 1970 and has served as Chairman of the Board of Trustees of Hamot Health Systems. Bob Merwin has served as Trustee of the First Christian Church and of Gannon University. He has also been active on the boards of the YMCA, ACES, the Manufacturers Association of Erie, Hiram College, the Erie Philharmonic, and the Hamot Medical Center. He served a six-year term on the Erie School Board and is a past president of the Erie Rotary Club. Together, Bob and Betty formed and direct the Merwin Foundation and in 1990 spearheaded the successful campaign to raise $1 million for the Erie Playhouse.

The Merwins have gained widespread recognition for their support of civic, cultural, social, educational, and medical organizations. Each has been awarded an honorary doctorate (Betty from Grove City College and Bob from Gannon University); each has been designated a Distinguished Pennsylvanian by the William Penn Society; and both were honored, along with Eriez, by the Erie Arts Council as recipients of the first Business/Arts Appreciation Award for their contributions to the arts dating back to the early 1940's. Bob has been chosen "Boss of the Year" by the Jaycees and Betty was selected in 1988 to receive Hiram College's Alumni Achievement Award "for her distinguished career in business and her civic leadership."

Both take great pride in the many Eriez employees who, over the years, have likewise contributed their services and financial support to countless

Bob and Betty Merwin.

charities and causes. The Erie area has been very fortunate to be home to a company with so many community-minded individuals in its employ.

As had O.F., Bob and Betty realized the importance of maintaining an honest and caring corporate environment. They also recognized that sound management skills and practices were vital to the health and progress of a company. When Bob took over the role of President of Eriez, he was acutely aware of his own lack of professional management training. He quickly set about to remedy that deficiency. One of his strongest attributes would turn out to be his willingness to admit he did not know everything and that he could learn a great deal from others. He was neither too arrogant nor too proud to ask for help or advice from anyone he thought could offer it.

In 1950 Bob went off to New York for a four-week training program run by the American Management Association. It would be the first of many contacts with the AMA. Two years later he joined the Young Presidents Organization, composed of young men and women who, before they turned forty, became presidents of companies with at least $1 million in sales. The knowledge they gained and the friends they made at the numerous YPO meetings they attended proved invaluable to both Bob and Betty. So involved in YPO did Bob become that he later was elected to its "graduate" organization, the Chief Executives Organization. A world-wide group now exceeding 1,000 presidents past the age of 49 who had been active in YPO, it included such members as Theodore Hesburgh, John Templeton and Winton Blount. His participation in AMA, YPO and CEO provided Bob with a constant flow of valuable ideas, information and advice. He picked up still more helpful knowledge at special courses at the Harvard Business School and Northwestern University.

Yet another important way the Merwins saw that they could broaden the knowledge and experience base of the company's management was by bringing prominent figures from outside the company onto its board of directors. Bob Merwin later explained his thinking in an article published in Nation's Business in 1982. Many private companies, he noted, limit their board membership to in-house executives and friends or relatives of the owner out of a concern for interference or criticism from outsiders. Reliance on such "rubber stamp" boards is shortsighted and harmful. "The wise executive," he wrote, "offsets his shortcomings with directors who are more experienced than he wherever the corporation needs good advice....Qualified directors can overcome the CEO's shortcomings in specific areas such as finance or manufacturing technology, as well as review corporate performance."

Early on, the Merwins recognized the value of the technical expertise, broad experience, and objective viewpoints that only outside directors could provide. In 1953 they took the first step to expand the Eriez Board of Directors beyond the Merwin family. In that year they added Edwin Nick, the former President of Copes-Vulcan and then Chairman of the Board of the Erie Insurance Exchange; Ralph Young, a Pittsburgh certified public accountant; and Thomas Doyle, a local attorney. In 1961 they made an important move to broaden even further the experience and expertise of the company's "outside" directors when Charles J. Webb and William E. Murphy joined the Eriez Board. Webb was President and Chairman of C.J. Webb, Inc. of Philadelphia and Murphy, a former associate of Charles Webb, was Executive Vice-President of the Mueller Company of Decatur, Illinois. Charlie Webb and Bill Murphy remain the longest-serving outside directors of Eriez and have provided tremendous service to the company over more than three decades.

In 1965 another key figure who is still active, Arthur F. Kroeger, was elected to the Board. A Harvard Business School graduate, Bud Kroeger headed an industrial consulting firm operating out of New York City (now headquartered in North Carolina) and served on the boards of dozens of other companies. Two other examples of the type of quality director Eriez succeeded in attracting to its Board in this period were Clifford Andrews and Dr. John C. Warner. Andrews, the Vice-President for Foreign Operations of the Ferro Corporation in Cleveland, brought important international experience to Eriez; Dr. Warner, former President of the Carnegie Institute of Technology and a renowned scientist, brought his considerable technological expertise to the Board.

The role that these and many other outside directors have played in the continued progress of Eriez cannot be stressed enough. As Bob Merwin has observed; "Without its experienced Board, Eriez would not have engaged in an aggressive growth program and earned its financial reputation." So impressed have the Merwins been with the advice and guidance they have provided that today outside directors outnumber their inside counterparts by six to four. The quality and the contributions of its outside directors have been and continue to be one of the major factors behind Eriez' success.

Based on his many efforts to broaden his own management education, coupled with expert guidance from the company's knowledgeable directors, Bob Merwin began to shape an enlightened management philosophy and to form an effective management team for Eriez. He created the Executive Management Committee to formulate and review short range operating plans and long range growth plans for the company. The Committee also set clear objectives for each department and division and acted to assure coordinated and cooperative interaction among them. To free top management to plan for profitable growth and to tap the energy and creativity of those below that level, Bob acted on the principle of delegating as much authority and responsibility down the line as possible.

If secondary supervision were to carry the responsibility for conducting current operations, Bob realized, then that responsibility could be effectively shouldered only if those supervisors were adequately informed and consulted. Too often, he noted, executives made the mistake of not recognizing that "People are the best assets of any company....they have ideas and knowledge which, if made available to management, can help the company better serve its customers. But often, nobody listens when people talk. Or nobody gives their 'people' a chance to talk. Their contributions are lost."

The Merwins determined this would not happen at Eriez. They took several steps to ensure that Eriez would be an "informed organization" whose leaders listened to and sought input from all employees. In addition to relying on publications such as <u>Magnetic Attractions</u> and <u>News from Eriez</u> (renamed <u>The Magnetic Link</u> in 1965), the company held regularly scheduled bi-monthly meetings at which reports were delivered on sales, profits, product development, production or service problems, activities of employee organizations, among other items. Questions and comments were encouraged.

The wives of Eriez representatives who attended the 1955 Sales Conference gather in front of the entrance to the Grove Drive office building.

Eriez opened yet another line of effective communication within the company when it created the Advisory Board. This Board has held a regular after hours dinner and meeting six times a year since its inception in 1959. Its twelve members are selected for three-year terms from the ranks of supervisors and other potential management candidates. A revolving membership system assures as wide a representation as possible and a continued influx of new ideas and fresh points of view.

The goals of the Eriez Advisory Board are threefold. One is to better acquaint middle-management personnel with overall company operations, plans and problems by presenting corporate and interdepartmental information in a more in-depth manner than can be achieved by memorandum or departmental meetings. Another is to enable individuals below major department head level to contribute ideas toward improvement of operations and profitability. Members are encouraged to offer their own ideas as well as to critique those presented to them by the President or a member of the Executive Management Committee. A final objective is to identify and develop managerial talent within the company. Over the past thirty years the Board has developed an impressive record of achievement in all these areas.

One of the major ideas the Merwins sought to communicate was that Eriez is a growth-oriented company not afraid of change. As one "Message from Management" in <u>Magnetic Attractions</u> put it: "Unless we remain flexible, adaptable, willing to accept and contribute to change, 'X' will mark the spot where we used to be, because we won't be there anymore. New, less rigid, more daring companies will be in our place...change is inevitable. It's up to us to use it, and make the most of it." This determination not to become self-satisfied and complacent, this willingness to explore new ideas and take risks, became important features of the Merwins' approach to management.

Only by appreciating the corporate culture the Merwins nurtured and the management philosophy they formulated can Eriez' emergence as the leader in its field be understood. Its rise to the status of recognized world authority took place during the ten years following O.F.'s death. In that decade the company brought forth an impressive array of new and improved products.

Eriez "bread and butter" product line in this period remained its broad array of permanent magnetic separators. A steady succession of improve-

ments to the original plate magnets, pulleys, drums and traps poured forth
from the company's engineering department. Customers could select from
an increasing variety of sizes, strengths and designs. They also found units
easier to install and clean as well as better protected from damage and
demagnetizing influences. In addition, several important new products were
developed, especially a series of tube-type grate magnets that came to be
widely used in the chemical and food processing industries.

First introduced in 1953, the grate magnet was ideal for removing
"tramp-iron" from free-flowing materials fed through hoppers, floor openings or closed vertical chutes. Eriez engineers arranged multiple small
Alnico castings to create a patented new magnetic circuit and encased them
in 1" diameter tubes. Several of these tubes were spaced an inch apart to form
a magnetic grate through which materials flowed. A steel grill placed just
above the spaces between the tubes served as a baffle to slow the material
flow and direct it onto the tubes. The wing-type grate magnet fit easily into
floor openings and hopper outlets, while a drawer-type unit was built for
installation in closed chutes and ducts. Both were soon available in "double-

An Eriez Grate Magnet, one of the many new products developed in the company's second decade.

bank" models with two rows of tubes to tackle the toughest fine iron removal jobs. The same innovative magnetic circuit design that made the grate magnet possible was also employed to dramatically improve the company's liquid traps.

To make its grates, traps and other separation equipment still more effective, Eriez constantly endeavored to increase the strength of the permanent magnetic materials it utilized. During this period new materials became available, especially ceramic magnets, that had certain advantages and disadvantages in comparison to Alnico. Since Eriez did not manufacture magnetic materials, it was not tied to the use of any one type. Rather, the company could rely on the considerable experience and skills of its engineers to determine which material could best be designed into a product for a specific purpose.

In 1957 Eriez marketed its first ceramic-based product, a low cost grate magnet for removing fine iron contaminants from thin material flows. Two years later, the company announced a new ceramic powered radial pulley. In 1960 Eriez introduced its new line of Series 17 plate magnets. These ceramic powered magnets offered greater pulling and holding power than ever before attained.

The company began advertising its new registered trade name, ERIUM, for the variety of "high quality permanent magnetic power sources, as specifically designed and energized by Eriez for use in Eriez equipment and components." Attention was called to Eriez' policy of "offering equipment which utilizes the best magnetic power source for your specific requirements at the most sensible cost to you." Eriez could boast of such a policy only because years of experience had made its sales and engineering people completely familiar with the characteristics and performance of all different types of permanent magnetic materials and equipment. This experience, coupled with the openness and flexibility of Eriez top management, enabled the company to be in the lead when the major shift from Alnico to ceramics took place in the 1960's.

All the activity directed at product improvement and new product development reflected the never-ending drive of Eriez personnel to find the most effective ways to use nonelectric magnetic separation devices to protect equipment from tramp iron damage and products from ferrous contamination. At the same time, similar efforts were also underway to broaden and improve the Eriez line of magnetic conveying equipment. The result of these efforts was a unique application of magnetic forces to the automation process that Eriez dubbed MAGNAmation (that is, magnets for automation).

During the 1950's a growing number of manufacturers sought to enter or progress in the "age of automation." Everyone looked for ways to simplify, accelerate, lower the cost of, and reduce the labor component in the production process. Special attention was paid to the handling of materials during that process. While Eriez did not design, build or sell material-handling systems, it did produce components and assemblies for such systems. Moreover, Eriez engineers worked closely with original equipment manufacturers or the direct users themselves to show how "magnetic action" could help them move materials faster, more economically, more efficiently, and more accurately.

In the metal working industries, for example, or wherever steel sheets were handled in piles, the Eriez Sheet Fanner greatly facilitated the feeding of individual sheets for stamping, punching, pressing or shearing operations. The Sheet Fanner induced the often sticky and sharp-edged sheets to repel one another and fan out for easy separation without prying or scratching.

The trend towards automation in the materials handling field provided Eriez with still another opportunity to broaden its product base. In a bold bid to branch into another field beyond magnetic separation or conveying, Eriez in 1956 unveiled its unique offering of vibratory feeders and bin vibrators. The tremendous success of its Hi-Vi line of equipment reflected the courageous, creative, and careful approach which Eriez brought to this risky move to diversify. The move was risky since Eriez would not be pioneering the field, as it did in permanent magnetic separation and conveying, but entering one where well-established suppliers already dominated the market. The success of the move, however, provided a strong boost to earnings and enhanced the company's reputation for imaginative research and creative engineering.

In 1955, concerned by the leveling off of separation equipment sales and convinced that Eriez' continued growth could best be assured by diversifying into new fields, the company engaged the services of the respected Arthur D. Little, Inc. consulting firm from Cambridge, Mass. The Little organization was asked to recommend a field in which Eriez could profitably engage, preferably one which required only a modest capital investment and in which the company's experience and reputation with processing industries could prove useful. It was also desirable that the product lend itself to distribution through the existing sales organization.

The Little report proposed that Eriez develop an advanced line of electromagnetic vibratory equipment consisting of vibratory feeders and unit (bin) vibrators. Vibratory feeders provided precise feeding, mixing and weighing of materials in amounts ranging from ounces to tons per hour. Food processors as well as chemical, cement, stone, ceramic, mining, and primary metals producers were large users of this type of equipment. Unit vibrators imparted a vibratory motion to bins, hoppers and chutes to prevent arching, sticking or packing of bulk materials being handled. Again, the food, chemical and mining industries used such equipment in many of their operations.

Eriez' management accepted the recommendation and immediately embarked on the formidable task of designing, engineering, producing and marketing a new product. The first step was to visit or send questionnaires to major users of vibratory feeders and bin vibrators to determine weaknesses in existing equipment and identify needed improvements. Eriez learned there were numerous problems: metal springs rusted and wore out; protection from dust and moisture were lacking; dead spots at the rear of trays and "front-end flip" at the discharge point interfered with controlled feeding rates; the design of some units prevented their use in tandem or back-to-back; and tuning controls were often cumbersome and imprecise. Above all, users complained about the need for inefficient, high maintenance current rectifiers to provide DC power to the electromagnetic drives.

Armed with this information, Eriez formed a four-man team led by Ronnie Hoff and Les Moskowitz to design superior models that eliminated these problems. Working out of the old 12th Street plant, they applied perseverance and ingenuity to develop within a year the first Hi-Vi feeders and vibrators. These radically improved units used less power, provided better linearity of feed, and had simpler, more accurate controls. Their new rustproof fiberglass springs and dust-tight aluminum covers made them more reliable and durable. The compact base of the feeder made it easier to use in combinations. The unit vibrator was designed to set up a double diaphragming or kneading action in the bin walls instead of merely hammering them with a series of blows like existing models.

The most innovative and important feature of the new models, however, was the patented motor drive mechanism that eliminated the need for a rectifier and could be directly plugged into any AC electrical outlet. Eriez' exclusive electro-permanent magnetic motor drive consisted of an electromagnet "E-frame" into the air gaps of which were inserted the legs of a U-shaped permanent magnet. The polarity of the electromagnet alternated with the line frequency while the polarity of the permanent magnet remained fixed. This set up a more efficient push-pull system than the pull-release system of simple electromagnetic units (see accompanying diagram.) This patented design dramatically reduced the power required to operate both mechanical and electromagnetic feeders. In 1958 the judges at the Design Engineering Awards Competition were so impressed with the new HI-VI Feeders that they honored Eriez for "Best Use of Materials in Product Design."

Eriez' initial feeders and vibrators were small units but within a few years

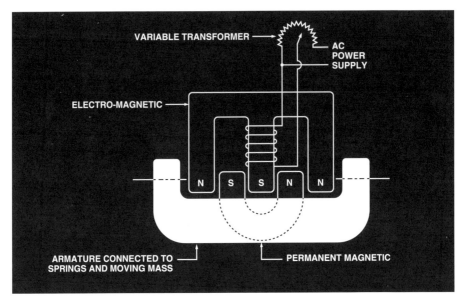

Eriez' patented Hi-Vi Magnetic Drive Circuit.

the company introduced a full line of models that permitted accurate feeding from a trickle of a few ounces per hour to a torrent of hundreds of tons per hour. To produce this new HI-VI line, Eriez expanded its work force by one-third.

At first, the sales of HI-VI equipment proved disappointing. The cost of Eriez units was higher than existing ones and many users preferred to wait and see how they performed over time. Gradually, however, Eriez learned to make its complex drives more economically and customers came to realize the superiority of HI-VI units. A major breakthrough came in 1960 when a California cement company ordered 135 Eriez feeders after its tests showed their advantages over competitive models in feeding consistency and power usage. Soon, sales to mining, rock products, chemical, food and primary metal markets began to climb rapidly.

Just as Eriez began to establish itself in the vibratory handling field, it made another significant move to expand into a new but still related area. This time the company decided to enter the electromagnetic separation equipment field, but by acquisition rather than by development of its own

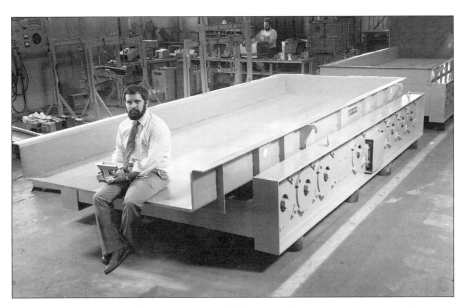

An Eriez employee holds one of the company's first Hi-Vi feeders while sitting on the tray of one of its largest mechanical feeders.

product line. In December, 1961 Eriez purchased the Magnetic Engineering and Manufacturing Company of Clifton, New Jersey.

Founded in 1940, MEMCO was one of the three largest producers of electromagnetic equipment in the country. Its acquisition provided Eriez with an extensive line of electromagnetic pulleys, drums and suspended magnets for heavy-duty separation jobs; wet drum separators and other special equipment for ore concentration and minerals beneficiation; electro lifting magnets for the steel industry and scrap yards; and magnetic sweepers for roadway, airport, and industrial use.

MEMCO enjoyed a reputation for outstanding electromagnetic engineering expertise. Many regarded its wet drum separators as the finest in the field and it had also pioneered the development of powerful oil-cooled suspended magnets. The combined technical experience of the two companies made available to Eriez customers greater magnetic engineering know-how than from any other single source.

MEMCO's powerful heavy-duty electromagnets were well known in the mining, power, pulp and paper, rock products, steel and reclamation industries. In some cases, especially involving ore concentration and minerals beneficiation, Eriez was entering areas for the first time. In other instances, it gained important additional contacts and experience in these fields. The company also acquired the services of some talented new personnel, especially John Lutton, who would make valuable contributions to Eriez' development.

The MEMCO addition made Eriez the world's largest producer of magnetic equipment for the processing industries. It also, as Bob Merwin noted at the time, "will provide us with a complete line for every application. We will be able to satisfy more of our customers' needs. Several new markets will open to Eriez. We gain in versatility and take another big step forward to continue the steady growth that has made Eriez the undisputed leader in the field."

Though not entirely evident at the time, ultimately as important to Eriez' growth as the acquisition of MEMCO and the development of the vibratory product line was the development of the company's first overseas operations. As in those other two instances, the story behind "Eriez Overseas" provides striking evidence of the vision, foresight and resource-fulness of the Merwins, their Board, and the company's top management.

As previously noted, Eriez began to export on a modest basis as early as 1944. As also noted, the Merwins early on recognized the potential of overseas markets for Eriez products. An Export Sales department was set up in 1948. Four years later the Eriez International Corporation was formed with the sole purpose of promoting sales abroad and investigating opportunities for overseas production. Vice-President Earl Miller and Export Manager Albert Stent devoted considerable attention and energy in Eriez' second decade to building its overseas business.

In several foreign markets Eriez faced mounting local competition and troublesome import duties and restrictions. Lacking large amounts of direct investment capital, the company explored the idea of granting manufacturing licenses to machinery companies in other countries to produce Eriez equipment in return for royalty payments. In the 1950's two such agreements were reached: with Toroid, Ltd. in Melbourne, Australia in 1954 and with a Paris-based affiliate of Acieries d'Ugine, a large steel producer, in France in 1958. The modest nature of the licensing fees received and the desire to be in direct control also led Eriez to pursue the preferred option of establishing subsidiaries abroad. During this period, the first two such subsidiaries emerged in Brazil and in Canada.

During his first Latin American trip in 1948, Bob Merwin had lined up a local company to import and distribute Eriez products in Brazil. Sales rose steadily until 1953, when they took a sharp drop as a result of new import restrictions. A return trip to the area plus consultation with McGraw-Hill's Overseas Business Services convinced Bob that the Brazilian market held great promise. Rather than cross off that market, he decided to set up an operation inside the country. In 1954 Imans Eriez do Brazil, Ltda., was created with a modest $60,000 investment and began producing Eriez equipment in Sao Paulo by the following April.

Almost immediately the new company's future was placed in jeopardy when the Brazilian government severely restricted imports of Alnico. The company scrambled to locate personnel and equipment to make its own castings. Suddenly, Eriez do Brazil was producing both Alnico and magnetic separators. When numerous representatives approached with requests to purchase sizable quantities of magnet castings, Bob Merwin recognized that the Alnico market in Brazil could prove quite profitable. He estimated, however, that it would take an additional $400,000 to expand the operation to tap that market.

Already committed to a significant investment in the vibratory endeavor, Bob Merwin was unwilling to give the Brazilian operation a financial guarantee from the parent organization. Instead, Bob set out to find risk capital to construct an expanded Alnico-producing facility at the Brazil plant. He found no financial interest in Cleveland or Pittsburgh, so he took his prospectus up and down Wall Street in the summer of 1955. Nearly twenty banks and investment houses concluded that "this is not the type of risk we are interested in." Undeterred, Bob always asked for suggestions as to who else might be. Someone suggested W.R. Grace & Co., which was just beginning to expand an operation in Brazil.

It took some temerity to approach this huge and internationally-experienced conglomerate with his prospectus, but Bob succeeded in interesting President Peter Grace. After further study, Grace recommended a more ambitious $1 million joint project in which his company would have 51% equity and active management participation. Reasoning that "we would rather have almost half of a sizable operation than nearly all of a small one," Bob agreed.

Peter R. Grace (right) meets with Betty Merwin and James Brydon during one of his several visits to Eriez.

A prospectus was drawn up offering $410,000 in stock and debentures in the new company. After failing to interest several underwriters in taking on the issue, Bob Merwin approached Charles J. Webb & Sons, an old, respected Philadelphia company familiar with foreign operations. Intrigued by the Grace connection and by Bob's demonstration with a plate magnet he brought with him, the Webbs agreed to visit Erie. Favorably impressed by the people and plant they saw, they offered to buy $300,000 of the stock and note package if the Merwin family would personally purchase the remaining $110,000. A handshake solidified the deal. Five years later, Charles J. Webb, Jr. began his nearly thirty years of service on the Eriez Board of Directors.

By 1958 the Eriez-Grace plant was producing both Alnico alloys and Eriez equipment in its new 40,000 square foot facility in an industrial park near Sao Paulo. While Eriez sold its 49% equity interest to Grace in 1962, it continued a licensing agreement with the company for the next decade and a half until, as we shall see, a new Brazilian subsidiary was formed.

Eriez emerged from its Brazilian ventures no longer an amateur in international operations. Contacts with the Grace organization and with foreign governments and companies, coupled with its decade-long efforts to promote sales abroad, provided Eriez' top management a perspective and experience uncommon in a company its size. In 1957 Robert Merwin presented a report to the International Management Association describing how Eriez began and expanded its world-wide operations. The Massachusetts Institute of Technology was so impressed with this story that it adopted the report as a case study for graduate students in International Management. Twelve years later M.I.T. updated what it came to consider a classic study on how a smaller company can successfully enter the international market.

To go with its licensees in Australia and France and its joint venture in Brazil, Eriez established its first wholly-owned subsidiary in Canada in 1961. Eriez' presence in Canada went back to 1946 when O.F. and Bob Merwin visited Toronto and selected the C.A. Richardson Company to sell Eriez products in Ontario. As the equipment line grew from a few plate separators to a full range of separation, conveying and vibratory equipment, so did Eriez' sales north of the border. So encouraged was the company by the response to its products in Canada that it soon looked to establish a manufacturing base there.

The right opportunity appeared when Soules Magnetics Ltd., a manufacturer of specialty magnetic products, became available for purchase. Eriez acquired Soules in 1961 and immediately moved into larger facilities in Downsview, a Toronto suburb. Eriez of Canada struggled through a difficult first couple of years until in 1963 Les Cramer, then acting as Office Sales Manager in Erie, was sent to take over as General Manager. Assisted by the able and affable Alf Mowat, Chief Engineer and Plant Manager, and the Gatt brothers, Steve and Bob, Cramer quickly had the company profitably producing a full line of Eriez products under the "Made in Canada" label.

As impressive for a small company as were these first steps into international markets, they were but an inkling of what was to come.

Equally as impressive was the quality of the management team Bob Merwin had assembled to guide Eriez into the future. Jim Brydon in Finance, Ned Hirt in Advertising, Earl Miller in International Operations, and Arlo Israelson in Engineering brought the benefits of experience, sound judgement, and hard work to their respective areas. As we shall soon see, a most valuable addition to this team was made in 1960 when a young executive named Chet Giermak was recruited to head up the company's marketing efforts.

In addition, during its second decade Eriez brought into its ranks a number of talented and dedicated people who would come to play prominent roles in the years ahead. Jim Torrey and Jim Floros in Engineering, Ed Twichell in Sales, Don Ross in Purchasing, Walt Cmiel in Customer Service, and Paul Chaffee in Accounting exemplify the leadership abilities found among so many of those who came to Eriez in this period.

With so much proven and emerging managerial talent in place, Eriez was well poised to meet the challenges of the decades ahead.

CHAPTER 3

STAYING AT THE TOP
1962-1991

"The secret of success
is constancy to purpose."

—Benjamin Disraeli

As difficult as it is to attain a position of preeminence in any field, sustaining such a position is even more of a challenge. Eriez Magnetics has proven equal to that challenge. Having reached the position of "world leader" in its field by the end of its second decade, Eriez has been able to retain its number one ranking over the past thirty years by maintaining and strengthening those same qualities that first brought it to the pinnacle of success.

Under the astute leadership of Bob and Betty Merwin, Chet Giermak and Richard Merwin, Eriez has continued to promote talented managers from within or to find them outside the company when necessary. A capable and dedicated workforce has constantly been recruited, retained, and forged into an efficient team. This team has continued to ensure that customers' problems are best solved by the quality products and service that Eriez delivers. New markets, both domestic and foreign, have been found. Always on the lookout for new technologies and novel applications, the company has maintained its reputation as an innovator rather than an imitator. Above all, Eriez management has never lost sight of the vision and values embodied in the company's Fundamental Principle.

As Eriez entered its third decade, one of the first things that had to be done to keep the company at the top was to provide adequate facilities for its rapidly expanding operations. By the late 1950s Bob Merwin recognized that the company was quickly outgrowing its Grove Drive home. In 1957 he enlisted Plant Engineer Al Allen to help search for a new site. After considering several alternatives, he settled two years later on the current Millcreek location, near the Erie airport. Ease of transportation is crucial for a company like Eriez with such far-flung markets and so many customers and employees traveling into and out of the area.

In 1959, the Merwins purchased the old Nicholson farm off Asbury Road just to the west of the Erie airport. With the support of the Greater Erie Industrial Development Corporation and the assistance of Millcreek Township officials who pledged to provide necessary roads, sewers and water, plans were drawn up for a new headquarters facility for Eriez on this 32 acre site. Over $1 million was invested in the construction of an 86,000 square foot complex to house production facilities, offices, and a modern test laboratory. Ground was broken in April, 1963. Under the watchful eye of Al Allen, construction proceeded so rapidly that only six months later, on November 23, 1963, dedication ceremonies were held and production in the new plant began.

Unlike the moves to West 12th Street in 1945 and Grove Drive in 1952, the shift to the Asbury Road location left Eriez with plenty of room for expansion. And it was not long before more room was necessary. A number of small expansions took place following the closing of the Clifton, N.J. plant in 1969 and the consolidation of all Eriez-Memco operations at the Erie facility. Continued growth through the 1970's required a major addition to the office portion of the main building in 1981. This expansion provided badly needed room not only for the Engineering Department and several main office occupants but also for an enlarged Progress Center to display Eriez products and host the mounting number of seminars and training sessions sponsored by the company.

Another section of the new headquarters complex that quickly needed expanding was the testing and research center. When it first opened in

1964, Eriez officials announced with pride that the Central Test Laboratory was the finest facility of its kind in the world. Eriez had always been known as a solver of problems not just a seller of products. Now the company could utilize the greatest array of magnetic, vibratory and conveying equipment available anywhere to tackle a wider range of materials processing and handling problems.

A wide variety of users soon challenged Eriez' experienced engineers and technicians to determine the most efficient and profitable way to process or handle a bewildering array of materials. Among those who have turned to the Central Test Laboratory for assistance are processors of all kinds of materials, especially ores, minerals, metals, chemicals and foods; equipment designers and manufacturers; government agencies; and organizations concerned with pollution and reclamation.

So great has been the demand for the lab's services over the past twenty-five years that the company has continually had to add space and equipment to the Eriez Technical Center, as it is now called. Major building additions have tripled the size of the complex that now houses its own library, computer room, conference center, sample storage area, dust-room, and three main testing areas. The Center's formidable arsenal of problem-solving weapons now numbers over 150 types of permanent magnetic, electromagnetic, vibratory, conveying and metal detecting equipment. This equipment ranges from simple plates, grates and traps to highly sophisticated devices such as a Rare Earth Roll Separator, an Eddy Current Separator and a Superconducting High Gradient Magnetic Separator System.

The Center receives a wide variety of samples from all over the world, along with requests for everything from a simple feasibility report to a complex pilot plant study. Since 1974 the annual number of material samples submitted for separation, purification or recycling tests has tripled to more than 600. Materials sent to the Center range from coffee to dog food, alumina to zircon, and crushed flashlight batteries to raw garbage. One of the more intriguing samples came from Lockheed Engineering and NASA, which sent simulated moon soil to be tested for the most effective way to concentrate ilmenite from crushed particles of the soil.

While the bulk of the testing involves materials separation, purification, concentration, or reclamation, problems involving materials movement and precise materials feeding are also handled. Recommendations are made not only about proper equipment and processes but also regarding the optimum quantity and rate at which materials should be treated or fed.

Tom Falconer, named Manager, Research & Development in 1971, ably directs operations at the Technical Center, while Marshall Carner serves as a most enterprising Supervisor of Research and Development. Joe Wernham oversees material testing activity. Thanks to their work and that of Eriez' other talented engineers and technicians, whenever anyone is in need of a way to effectively separate, purify, concentrate, move, feed or recover materials of any kind they usually turn to Eriez for advice. It is this reputation that brings nearly 200 visitors a year from around the world to Eriez' World Headquarters.

The Eriez Technical Center - *A view of the main testing room.*

Research & Development/ Engineering Personnel*: (left to right): Marshall Carner, Joe Wernham, Jerry Rose, Dick Darling, Tom Falconer.*

The steady expansion of the Technical Center, as well as the office and production areas, is testimony to the healthy growth that the company has enjoyed over the past thirty years. Fortunately for Eriez, the Board of Directors had the foresight in 1959 to acquire a tract of land sufficient to accommodate that growth.

Not long after he made the commitment to acquire the Asbury site, Bob Merwin took an even more important step to bolster the future of the company. Looking to replace Dick Roosevelt, who resigned after a decade of service as Sales Manager and moved to California to handle Eriez' products, Bob traveled to Chicago to interview a dynamic and personable young executive named Chester F. Giermak. The decision to invite Giermak to join the Eriez team in July, 1960 was one of the most fortuitous ones in the company's history.

Giermak graduated from William and Mary with a degree in economics.

Following stints with General Motors in Dayton and Johnson and Johnson in Chicago, he joined the Stephens-Adamson Company, later an Allis Chalmers' subsidiary. After establishing and directing a new marketing department at the Aurora, Illinois-based company, he was named General Manager of the Standard Products Division and Assistant to the Executive Vice President.

After nearly nine years with the company, Giermak began looking for new opportunities. When he met Bob Merwin in Chicago on his search for a new Sales Manager, the fit seemed perfect. Eriez needed someone with Giermak's experience and vitality; he wanted to join a company that shared his values and management philosophy.

On the first of several trips to Erie that followed the initial meeting, Giermak was surprised at Eriez' relatively small size. Based on its extensive advertising and promotional campaign, he expected to find a much larger company. He was, however, attracted by the philosophy upon which the company had been founded and the corporate culture it had developed. He saw an ethical company that dealt honestly with and truly cared about its associates, its customers, its suppliers and its community. The decision was not difficult. He readily accepted Bob Merwin's offer to become Assistant to the President at Eriez.

Chet Giermak

A rapid series of promotions soon followed. In November, 1960 Giermak was named Sales Manager. Two years later he became Director of Marketing for all divisions and subsidiaries. Appointment as Vice President, Marketing came the following year. In 1969 the company announced that he would fill the newly created position of Executive Vice President and General Manager. On January 1, 1971 Chet Giermak was named President and Chief Executive Officer of Eriez. Bob Merwin, as Chairman of the Board, now concentrated on acquisition of new products and companies, expanding international operations, and long range planning.

The decision to turn over the operational reins of the company to Chet Giermak was based on the outstanding performance of the sales and marketing team under his direction and on the recognition that he possessed the essential personal attributes to provide sound and humane management in keeping with Eriez' Fundamental Principle. The wisdom of this judgment was attested to by the outstanding progress the company made during the two decades of his leadership. Sales jumped from $8.2 million in 1971 to over $50 million in 1990, virtually all the result of internally generated new and improved products; the company remained in the forefront of the magnetic processing equipment industry; and, most importantly, Eriez' corporate culture of integrity, caring and pride has been strengthened.

Like the Merwins, Giermak has been highly active in both industry organizations and community affairs. A past president of the Processing Equipment Manufacturers Association, he has also served as a director of the National Association of Manufacturers. Locally, he has been active in ACES (Americans for the Competitive Enterprise System) and the Sales and Marketing Executives Club of Erie. He is a board member and past president of both the Erie Conference on Community Development and the Manufacturers Association of Northwest Pennsylvania. He also serves on the Board of Directors of Erie Press Systems. A member of the Fellowship of Christian Athletes, he is a corporator of Hamot Medical Center and trustee and past president of the Saint Vincent Foundation for Health and Human Services.

Clearly, this extensive involvement in outside activities has not come at Eriez' expense. Giermak has been able to maintain a vital presence at the company. His active, hands-on managerial style leads him to wander through the offices and plant on an almost daily basis talking with as many employees as possible. "Chet", as he is commonly referred to by Eriez employees, is certainly no aloof or distant CEO known only by his picture in the annual report. Able to address every employee by name, he maintains an "open door" policy that encourages any company member to come in and discuss any issue with him at any time. This policy exemplifies one of the least tangible but most important contributions Chet Giermak has made to Eriez: the solidification of the company character first shaped by the Merwins in the company's formative years.

A wide variety of employee improvement programs has been offered from first-aid instruction to blueprint reading classes and from financial planning sessions to pre-retirement seminars. Recently the company announced a free counseling program to help employees and their family members deal with personal problems. Concern about the health and safety of workers led the company in 1982 to begin a ten-year program to first limit and then eliminate smoking at Eriez. In 1986 the company initiated a policy of hiring only non-smokers and in 1990 announced there would be a completely smoke-free environment at the company by July 1, 1992. The company offers to pay the costs for smokers and their spouses who need help to quit smoking.

Along with the respect he accords every employee, Giermak also treats them with an uncommon degree of trust. He ordered time clocks removed "as a way of saying to our people that we trust them to arrive and leave at designated times." He then removed all bells and buzzers that signaled coffee breaks "in Pavlovian fashion." He also eliminated the mandatory vacation during summer shut-down. Based on the belief that "every individual should determine his or her own vacation schedule," vacations can now be taken at any time throughout the year.

How have Eriez personnel responded to a culture that says "we trust and respect you?" Rather than abuse the trust, people started showing up for work early. Eriez has an absenteeism rate less than one-quarter the national average and pilferage is virtually nonexistent. Company loyalty is very high. The turnover rate is abnormally low.

The staunch loyalty of Eriez employees is reflected in the growing membership of the Pioneer Club. The club is an informal group of the longest-standing Eriez workers that began in 1960. It is open to men with at least 25 years and women with at least 15 years of service at Eriez. It currently has 84 members, almost two-thirds of them still active with the company.

Productivity and quality of workmanship have been such that Eriez has been profitable in each of the past thirty years except for the severe recession year of 1983. As the <u>Magnetic Link</u> put it: "At Eriez Magnetics we have our priorities in order. We put people ahead of profits and, in turn, we have good people and we have good profits."

The company has always shown the same concern for its customers that it has for its employees. In the words of Alf Mowat, former plant manager of Eriez of Canada: "Eriez has always been an honest and honorable company. It doesn't let people down. And it covers its mistakes instead of trying to cover them up."

Over the past two decades several efforts have been mounted to make Eriez even more of a "customer-oriented" company. In 1971 a Quality Assurance Department was established, well before the concept became so popular. That same year the Customer Service Department was created to provide prompt, efficient field service for all Eriez products.

Under the direction of Walt Cmiel, the Customer Service Department provided far more than just "run-of-the-mill" service. In Arlo Israelson's words, whether it be a matter involving product selection, installation, operation or maintenance: "It doesn't matter where in the world he is or what time it is – when a customer needs help, the people from Eriez Magnetics are ready to give it." Eriez sales representatives are especially appreciative of this service. As one of the company's newer sales represen-tatives commented recently: "The willingness of Eriez to work with customers and satisfy their needs proves more powerful than the magnets themselves." Yet another noted: "The true measure of the manufacturer is not necessarily how it reacts in a sales situation, but how it reacts in a crisis. We haven't had one instance where Eriez was not more than willing to go the extra mile...in order to ultimately satisfy our customers."

Senior Office Personnel: *seated (left to right): Annie Zenor, Mary Skellie; standing: Pat Monahan, Kathy Williams, Chris Ducharme, Geri Baker; absent: Marge Kurtich and Marilyn Dennen.*

Numerous market surveys support the image of Eriez as a quality service company. Indeed, one independent research firm commented after a survey it conducted: "Eriez Magnetics comes out with one of the most positive market approvals we have ever encountered in a study of this type...and Eriez came in with one of the highest ratings we've ever seen in keeping its promises." Anxious to retain that approval, the company pushed to improve performance in an area where it felt it could do better – on-time shipments.

In 1981 Eriez instituted a new program called UNICUS (Unified System for Customer Service). Computerized control of inventory, procurement, scheduling and manufacturing processes resulted in substantial improvement in the order fulfillment system. In 1987 Eriez launched its 'RIGHT. ON TIME.' campaign, which stressed the importance of not only when a product was shipped but also its quality. As the <u>Magnetic</u> <u>Link</u> described the new program: "The 'right' means Eriez quality and that <u>all</u> specifications of the shipped product will exactly match the original order. 'On time' means what it says, to the day." Eriez now ships almost 90% of its orders on the specified date.

Before respected and motivated employees can deliver quality, on-time products and superior service to satisfied customers, those customers have to first be aware that those products and services exist and can meet their needs. Again in this area, as in so many others, Eriez benefitted from the fact that during its first twenty years Bob Merwin, assisted by Dick Roosevelt, Ned Hirt and Arlo Israelson, had moved the company ahead of its competitors.

Production Supervisors: *(left to right): John Lutton, Don Ross, Fred Adams, George Rohleder.*

Quality Control Supervisors: *(left to right):* Jeff Kiehl, Ray Cook.

Customer Service Personnel: *seated:* Mike Kosteniuk; *standing (left to right):* Myron Pifer,
David Hanson, Jerry Newell.

In terms of the impact and extent of its advertising and promotions as well as the quality and experience of its sales representatives, Eriez stood head and shoulders above the field almost from the start. Over the past twenty years, thanks to the strong leadership provided by Ed Twichell in Sales and first Dave McHenry and now Keith Jones in Advertising, Eriez has remained the best in the industry with regards to advertising, marketing, and sales force.

Eriez' rich advertising tradition has been further strengthened by its association since 1979 with the firm of Dix & Eaton, Inc. Under the guidance of Ed Stevens, Group President, Dix & Eaton (Erie) has helped to develop and coordinate an effective, multifaceted program to stimulate interest in Eriez products and generate leads for its sales people.

The company has never relied on advertising alone to attract prospective customers. Eriez products have been highlighted at numerous national and international trade shows since the late 1940s. In the 1960s and early 1970s the company even staged its own traveling trade show. "By-

Marketing Personnel: *seated (left to right): Ed Razanauskas, Ed Twichell, Bill Bules; standing: Dan Norrgran, Don Dennen, Keith Jones, Al Gedgaudas, Mike Latimer.*

invitation-only" MAGNAramas featuring the latest in Eriez products were held in cities across the country, from Birmingham to Detroit and St. Louis to Boston. Also shown to a wide variety of audiences have been the several films Eriez has made to explain its many products and exemplify their numerous uses.

Since the mid-1960s Eriez has also sponsored a number of important and well-attended forums and conferences dealing with recent developments and important issues in its many fields of interest. In 1964 Bob Merwin organized the first Eriez Magnetics Executive Forum. Designed as a means of exchanging ideas and information, the Forum attracted over one hundred representatives from business, industry, government agencies, research firms and universities anxious to hear and talk about new advances in magnetic and other technologies. More such forums followed in later years.

Eriez also holds periodic product application seminars that attract representatives from around the world. Most successful have been its Ore

Eriez representatives from around the world gather to attend a Sales Conference.

Treatment Conferences and its Forum on Paramagnetic Separation. In addition to these formal meetings, Eriez regularly welcomes to its headquarters facility a host of annual visitors interested in learning more about some aspect of its work. In 1990, for example, thirty-five Quality Assurance and Engineering personnel from ten top food plants around the country came to Erie to learn more about applications for their company's magnetic separation and metal detection equipment.

While ads, trade shows, conferences and visits can lead to awareness, interest and, hopefully, inquiries, it takes an experienced, knowledgeable and persuasive sales force to translate those inquiries into orders. The network of independent and in-house sales personnel that Eriez has built up around the country and the world is without parallel in the field. Of the more than thirty field offices around the country, eight are district offices directly staffed by Eriez personnel (Philadelphia, Chicago, New York, Detroit, Pittsburgh, Boston, Houston and Baltimore.) While the company prefers to rely on independent sales representatives whenever possible, it has created its own offices in these major urban areas when previously appointed independent sales representation was unable to assure satisfactory coverage.

Crucial to the effectiveness of this carefully-selected, talented and loyal group of sales representatives has been Eriez' extensive program of education, training and information sharing. Important news, ideas, tips and experiences are shared with everyone in the network through regular bulletins, newsletters and announcements. And standing ready to help in any way possible is the entire force of headquarters personnel.

One of the most important reasons Eriez sales people are the best-trained and most knowledgeable in the industry is the International Sales Conference program. Held every other year, these conferences bring over one hundred field sales office personnel from the United States and around the world to Eriez headquarters to learn about new products and applications and to exchange valuable ideas and information. The fun and good fellowship shared at these meetings results in a bond of respect, cooperation and loyalty between the company and its associated sales personnel.

In the highly competitive and rapidly changing environment in which Eriez operates, Bob Merwin recognized that to insure the company's future a strong and active Board of Directors had to be maintained. Thus, to the helpful guidance that continued to be provided by such veteran members as Charles Webb, William Murphy, and Arthur (Bud) Kroeger was added the wise counsel of several new voices, especially those of John E. Britton, A. James Freeman, John H. Hubbard, and Richard A. Merwin.

Appointed to the Board in 1972, Attorney John Britton brings valuable legal counsel to the company. A Harvard Law School graduate and partner in the prestigious local firm of MacDonald, Illig, Jones and Britton, he also contributes insights gained from his service on the boards of several other companies. Jim Freeman, vice chairman and former president of Lord Corporation, joined Eriez' Board in 1985. A Chemical Engineering graduate of Northeastern University, he brings years of extensive experience in industry to Board meetings. Jack Hubbard, a member of the Board since 1986, likewise provides guidance based on years of experience in the metrology/machine tool industry. Holder of a master's degree in Industrial Management from MIT and former president of Coherent General Inc. of Sturbridge, Mass., Hubbard was recently named president of Federal Products Co., a leading manufacturer of high precision analog and digital measurement and inspection instruments.

It was a happy day when Richard Merwin, the son of Bob and Betty Merwin, joined the Eriez team. After graduating from Stanford University, Richard took a position with the Economic Development Administration of the U.S. Department of Commerce. Bilingual and a world traveler, he became Licensee Coordinator in the Eriez International Division in 1966.

Upon his arrival at the company Richard saw that "the international market offers one of the greatest growth potentials open to Eriez." His language skills and intense interest in other peoples and cultures naturally inclined him to focus his activity on the company's overseas markets. As

General Manager of the International Division in the period 1974-80, and as Vice-President, International from 1980-86, Richard helped make sales and profits from international markets a vital part of the company's health. As we shall soon see, he played an especially prominent role in establishing Eriez' strong network of overseas affiliates.

The Eriez Board of Directors: seated (left to right): Robert F. Merwin, Betty M. Merwin, Richard A. Merwin, Chester F. Giermak; standing (left to right): William E. Murphy, Jack H. Hubbard, Arthur F. Kroeger, Charles J. Webb, II, Paul V. Chaffee, A. James Freeman, John E. Britton.

Elected to the Board of Directors in 1978, Richard was named Chairman of that body in 1986. This appointment symbolized the Merwin's determination to keep Eriez a family-held company committed to its employees and the Erie community. It also brought to the Chairman's helm a wealth of international knowledge and experience that have proved crucial for a world-oriented company like Eriez. As Chairman, Richard has focused his efforts on corporate planning, especially abroad, and the growing mining and minerals fields that offer considerable potential for Eriez equipment and services.

Currently, he is a member of the American Institute of Mining,

Richard A. Merwin

Metallurgical and Petroleum Engineers and the International Trade Executive Club. He is also a director of the Erie Metropolitan YMCA and a member of the Council of Fellows at the Behrend Campus of Penn State University.

Under the leadership of Bob, Betty, and Richard Merwin, together with the astute guidance from Treasurers James K. Brydon, Jr., Paul V. Chaffee, and now Dennis Salsbury, the Board of Directors has played an essential role in helping Eriez maintain a strong financial condition. The Board also strongly supported one of the most important decisions of this period—the commitment to further diversify Eriez in terms of product, market, and geographic area.

Thanks to Bob and Betty Merwins' foresight and efforts, Eriez had never really been a one product, one industry, one market-area company. From the introduction of the first pulleys and drums in the late 1940s through the development of the conveying and vibratory lines in the 1950s to the acquisition of MEMCO's electromagnetic equipment in 1961, Eriez had built its leadership position on the development of a diverse array of products. And ever since that down-state trip in 1945 revealed the variety of potential customers for Eriez separation equipment, the Merwins endeavored to expand the number of industries in which Eriez products were utilized. Through their own frequent travels and the creation of a network of national and international sales representatives they also made clear their determination to see Eriez products distributed on as widespread a basis as possible. Over the past thirty years this rich diversity of products developed, markets serviced, and areas operated in has grown even further. Such diversification has come close to making Eriez if not "recession-proof" then at least "recession-resistant."

Eriez' strategy of diversifying its product line over the past three decades has been achieved internally through fruitful research and development efforts and externally through carefully selected acquisitions. The separation, conveying and vibratory lines have been greatly expanded and strengthened through product development while new screen separation and metal detection equipment lines have been added.

In the separation area, which remains the company's largest sales volume producer, a host of new and improved products have been introduced. The new self-cleaning grates, first unveiled in 1971 and recently automated, won an award from Food Processing magazine for "significant contribution to the industry." Important improvements and additions have been made to the line of suspended electromagnets inherited from MEMCO in 1961. Eriez was also the first to develop suspended permanent magnets as powerful as electromagnets but without the operating costs and problems caused by power failures.

The most significant innovation in the separation area, however, was not a new product but a new material. In the mid-1980s Eriez became the first in its industry to use new rare earth magnetic materials (especially neodymium-boron-iron alloys) in some of its plates, grates, traps and drums. Up to twenty-five times stronger than their ceramic magnet counterparts, these new Erium Super Strength Rare Earth models have proven ideal for removing fine iron and weakly magnetic materials from all types of wet or dry free-flowing products. As we shall see in a moment, a number of other important separation products have been developed to meet customer needs in two rapidly growing market areas—ore treatment and reclamation.

In the materials movement and handling field the original MAGNAmation rails, rolls and racks have been supplemented by a collection of versatile lifting magnets. From lightweight Selectos to heavy-duty circular and rectangular electros, used singly or in groups, Eriez now offers a tremendous variety of magnets to lift, transfer, position, pile or unpile steel and iron of all shapes and sizes. One of its unique offerings is the Safehold Permanent Magnet that can be turned on and off like an electromagnet but will not drop its load in the event of a power failure.

Finance Personnel: *seated: Dennis Salisbury; standing (left to right): Troy Fensel, Karen Banaszek, Dave Meyer, Kathy Williams.*

Two other important additions to the MAGNAmation line have been the Chip and Parts Conveyor and the Coolant Cleaner, both of which have found ready markets in the metalworking industry since their introduction in 1970. By moving products from tiny washers to parts weighing hundreds of pounds or by removing unwanted by-products of the machining process like chips, grindings or slugs, the Eriez patented Chip and Parts Conveyors can speed up production rates appreciably. Their liquid-tight construction permits them to be immersed in tanks. The Eriez Coolant Cleaner removes iron contamination from coolant fluid, thereby reducing coolant costs and lengthening the life of cutting tools, grinding wheels and pumps in which the coolants are used.

Eriez has also continued to strengthen its steadily growing vibratory line. With their unique electro-permanent magnetic motor drive, Eriez light and high speed medium-duty vibratory feeders for mixing, weighing and packaging equipment had come to dominate the market. While improvements to these electromagnetic feeders have continued to be made, especially to the high-speed and the heavy-duty models, the emphasis in recent years has been on expanding Eriez' role in the materials feeding field by the development of mechanical feeders and conveyors used in medium and heavy industries. Eriez now offers a full range of heavy-duty mechanical vibrating feeders to move large volumes of bulk materials (up to 2800 tons per hour) in the mining, pulp and paper, stone and gravel, chemical processing and scrap industries. Eriez feeders also now come with a tremendous variety of trays, screens, covers, liners and coatings. To move materials over long distances the company recently brought out a single-mass mechanical conveyor for light materials such as foods and chemicals and a two-mass conveyor for high volumes of bulk materials.

Eriez' leadership position had been built on the variety and quality of its separation, conveying and vibratory products. Its position has been maintained not only by adding to the variety and improving the quality of its equipment for these three fields but also by moving into new product areas as well.

In 1971 the Board of Directors approved the purchase of a line of vibratory screens and vibratory conveyors from the Syncro-Matic Division of State Steel Products Company of Industry, California. Not long after acquiring Syncro-Matic, Eriez developed a new Syncro-Sizer dry screen separator to more effectively sift dry materials to insure a more uniformly sized end product. Recently, movement has been made into the promising field of rectangular screen separators for scalping, dedusting and cutting.

An important addition to Eriez came with the acquisition of a line of metal detectors that can signal the presence of non-magnetic metals in food products, chemicals, rubber, wood and other materials requiring processing. Eriez had briefly flirted with this market in the early 1950s but quickly left it when it became apparent that equipment of that day lacked the necessary sensitivity and reliability. As increasingly more sophisticated equipment was developed over the years, Eriez decided to get back in the business.

In 1981 Eriez purchased a line of metal detectors from International Telephone and Telegraph and set up a division that was soon marketing advanced products that could be sold along with Eriez equipment for removal of ferrous metal impurities. The Series 1200 detectors were ideal for use with such materials as magnetic ores, coal, aggregates and logs. Another

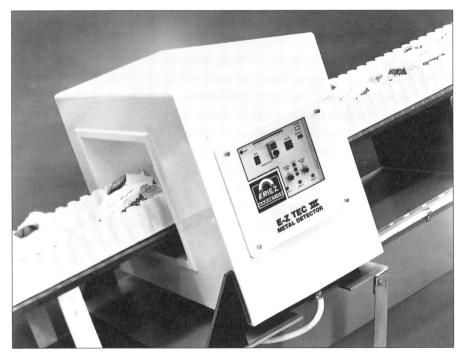

Bags of potatoes pass through the aperture of the E-Z Tech III Metal Detector to protect against unwanted tramp metal.

line was designed to provide a machine capable of detecting very small metallic particles. The most recent version can detect ferrous and non-ferrous particles in the one-half millimeter range in dry or wet conductive products. Designed for the cosmetic, pharmaceutical, textile and plastics industries, these machines can be used not only to detect metals that must be removed to protect equipment or insure product purity but also to assure that they are present (for example, the little metal ties in packages of plastic garbage bags.) With sales rapidly climbing, Eriez in 1989 constructed a special climate-controlled room with an anti-static floor and electrostatic air cleaner for assembly and testing of the detectors with their extremely sensitive solid-state electronics.

With such a rich variety of products, available in so many types and sizes and suitable to solve an incredible range of materials processing problems, Eriez is in the fortunate position of servicing a tremendous number of very diverse industries. The largest single segment of Eriez' broad customer base is the food industry, which accounts for approximately 15% of total sales. While the chemical, mining, paper, metalworking, and stone/clay/glass products industries all represent important markets for Eriez, it takes customers in more than twenty Standard Industrial Classifications to reach the 90% of sales level.

Following the example set by Bob Merwin in the 1940s when he set out to find new users in the textile, food and chemical industries to go along with the original feed grain and milling customers, Eriez continues to look for novel applications for its separation, conveying, feeding, screening, and metal detecting equipment in still more markets. In the last couple of decades particularly fruitful ground for Eriez' efforts to cultivate new customers has been found in two areas—ore and mineral treatment and pollution control.

Sales to users of Eriez products in the ore treatment field have grown so rapidly that ten years ago a separate Ore Treatment Division was established. The company's entry into this market came by way of the magnetic wet drum separators manufactured for the beneficiation of iron ores. Since then, however, Eriez has produced a number of low-intensity and high-intensity separation devices that very effectively recover or remove magnetic materials from a variety of ores and minerals. New permanent and electro-permanent type wet drums proved highly efficient at separating weakly magnetic materials from slurried feeds. To treat feebly magnetic materials that do not respond well to traditional methods of processing on low intensity wet drum separators, Eriez developed increasingly stronger and higher capacity Wet High Intensity Magnetic Separators (WHIMS). A high-intensity Induced Magnetic Roll (IMR) Separator performed the same function for dry materials.

Over the last decade the demand has mounted for high-purity materials used in the manufacture of items such as specialty ceramic and electrical components, insulators, substrates, adhesives, specialty glass and fiberglass, optical fibers, and alloys. To remove even trace amounts of feebly magnetic particles from such materials Eriez offers the recently developed Rare Earth Roll Separator and the High Intensity Dry Vibrating Filter. The RE Roll, for example, can magnetically clean silica sand and feldspar to glassmaking quality. The Dry Filter, with its unique vibrating action and powerful high-gradient magnetic matrix, is excellent for treating very fine dry particle streams of alumina, magnesia, talc, and silica and zircon flours. Eriez' High Gradient Magnetic Separator (HGMS), with its tremendously powerful field of up to 20,000 gauss, can take on the toughest purification jobs such as removing even submicron size paramagnetic particles from materials like kaolin clay, used in ceramics, paints, inks, plastics, and to coat printing papers.

Pollution control is another area Eriez began to see the importance of and opportunities in as early as the 1960s. As concern about the polluting of our air, water and land grew in that decade, Eriez quickly became active in all three areas. The company's experience as a solver of separation problems of all types made it well-suited to tackle many of our serious environmental challenges. As Bob Merwin noted in 1967: "Actually, most pollution abatement work involves separation of one material from another...separation of dust and fly ash from air, separation of unwanted solids from water, or separation of valuable elements from solid waste."

The largest Eriez Refuse Magnetic Separator ever built is being used in a waste reclamation application at LaCrosse, Wisconsin.

One of Eriez' first steps into the pollution control area came in 1969 with the development of an electrostatic knocker or rapper designed to shake into collection hoppers the dust collected by electrostatic precipitators used in smoke abatement equipment. Manufacturers of such equipment soon made Eriez Precipitator Vibrators a standard feature of their products.

It now appears that Eriez' most prominent role in the pollution control arena will be played in the solid waste management and resource recovery fields. More than two decades ago Eriez designed an efficient system for separating desired metals from unwanted non-metallics in automobile shredding or maceration plants. Its powerful suspended magnets, recently incorporated into the dramatically effective Refuse Separators, have long been used to separate ferrous materials from municipal waste and in other recycling processes. In 1976 Eriez introduced an electrostatic separator that exploits differences in conductivity to separate conductors from non-conductors and various non-magnetic metals, such as aluminum, copper and brass from one another.

Probably no other company in the world produces as many products applicable to the waste management process as does Eriez. Trash shredders need magnetic protection from tramp iron; trash hoppers need bin vibrators; trash movement requires vibratory feeders and conveyors. Trash separation requires suspended electro or permanent magnets, magnetic pulleys and drums, screens, and eddy-current separators. More and more automated waste management plants around the country are finding that Eriez is best suited to incorporate such equipment into an efficient system.

At the same time that Eriez was moving into the ore treatment and reclamation markets, it was also acting to further spread the geographic base of its operations. As the <u>Magnetic Link</u> once noted: "It wasn't by staying at home that Eriez earned its reputation as 'world' authority." Bob and Betty Merwin's early initiatives to promote export sales and to establish overseas manufacturing locations provided a valuable base on which Eriez has steadily built for the past thirty years.

Today, the International Division, under the direction of Richard Merwin, sells Eriez products in virtually every country from Austria to Zaire. In addition, Eriez now has manufacturing facilities in seven countries on five continents. Just as the diversity of industries serviced insulate the company from downturns in any one market, this expansion of overseas sales and operations shelters it from the effects of recession in any one country or region. It also positions Eriez to take advantage of growth opportunities almost anywhere.

Eriez started selling abroad shortly after it began operations. Long before

Cuni Johannesen raises the "E" for excellence flag awarded to Eriez by President Johnson for the company's outstanding record in developing export sales.

other companies recognized the importance of international marketing, Eriez was advertising in international trade journals, attending international trade shows and signing up sales representatives abroad.

So successful were its early efforts to foster overseas sales that in 1965 Eriez was honored by the Department of Commerce with the President's "E"

Award for its substantial contribution to expanding America's export trade. In awarding Eriez the flag and certificate symbolizing its achievement of "excellence," Secretary of Commerce John O'Conner praised the company for its "initiative, resourcefulness and follow-through...in energetically cultivating markets around the world." He noted that its accomplishments "reflect credit on management, employees and the Free Enterprise System."

Pleased as he was with the increasing sales abroad of "made in Erie" products, Bob Merwin saw that a combination of preferences, trade barriers and economic advantages from domestic production made the establishment of direct manufacturing facilities a necessity in certain countries and regions. Thus, in the 1960s and 1970s he and Betty traveled extensively around the globe seeking first new licensing agreements, then joint-venture projects, and, finally, acquisition of wholly-owned subsidiaries.

Additional licensees were lined up for a time in South Africa in 1964 and in the United Kingdom in 1967. By the late 1960s the company felt financially secure enough to explore two joint-venture opportunities. In the period 1974-1980 efforts spearheaded by Richard Merwin led to the establishment of five Eriez-owned affiliates.

Eriez set up its first joint-venture in Japan. Following an overture from a couple of Japanese firms, Bob and Betty Merwin made an extended trip to Tokyo in 1967 to explore a business partnership with the Taiko Trading Company, its sales representative in Japan since 1963, along with Japan Special Steel and Mitsubishi Steel Manufacturing. Two years of discussions culminated in 1969 with the formation of Eriez-Japan, which brought together the magnetic technologies of Eriez and the sales capabilities of Taiko. Eriez held 40% of the stock. Its Japanese partners provided financial, production and marketing management.

Eriez second joint-venture arose in Mexico. Sales of Eriez products in that country date back to the mid-1940s. Over the years it became increasingly evident that local production of Eriez equipment would enhance opportunities for sales expansion not only in Mexico but in Central

America as well. Hence, in 1972 Eriez joined with Equipos de Proceso, its Mexican sales representative since 1960, to form Eriez Equipos Magneticos, S.A. With Eriez limited by Mexican law at the time to less than 50% ownership, majority control rested with Equipos de Proceso, whose head, Vincent Carreto de la Mora, became President of the Mexican operation. Al Stent, Eriez International Division Manager at the time, played a major role in the formation of this new joint-venture.

While such joint-ventures were preferable to the licensing agreements pursued earlier, Eriez still desired affiliates based on the Eriez-Canada model of 1961. During the 1970s it consciously sought to gain full ownership and control over all but one of its overseas operations. This movement coincided with the emergence of Richard Merwin as the guiding force behind Eriez' International Division. Richard was convinced that the company's international activities could play an increasingly prominent role in its growth and would be one of the keys to the retention of its leadership position. Assisted by Mike Morales and Paul Hopsecger, Richard led the International Division to an impressive record of growth in export sales. He also took the lead in creating several of the wholly-owned subsidiaries that emerged in this period.

In Japan things had not gone well for Eriez and its partners almost from the start. Poor management and a board divided over a program of action led to losses or only breakeven operations. Everyone agreed that Eriez-Japan would not get into a profit position under divided management. The partners consented to turn over management to Tadashi Homma, who had sold Eriez products for Taiko since 1965. The Japanese partners also expressed an interest in selling their equity interest to Eriez. After a long period of negotiations in Japan, Richard Merwin in 1974 worked out an agreement whereby Eriez would acquire majority control immediately and total ownership by 1979. With Homma staying on as manager, an abrupt turnaround occurred. Eriez-Japan not only saw sales jump from $566,000 in 1974 to more than $6 million in 1990 but it eliminated all its debt as well.

As a result of successful negotiations conducted by Eriez vice-president James Brydon and Chet Giermak, Eriez acquired the assets of its licensee in the United Kingdom in 1974. Fred Downie was named general manager of the Eriez-U.K. operation in Caerphilly, Wales. Downie continues in this role today, though the plant location has been moved once again and the name changed to Eriez-Europe, symbolizing its anticipation of the full implementation of the European Economic Community in 1992.

Another former licensee soon followed in these footsteps. In 1977 Eriez Magnetics Pty., Limited, the company's licensee in Australia, was purchased outright by Eriez. Richard Merwin serves as President and Ron Poole, a veteran of Eriez operations in Australia, as General Manager.

Problems with licensee-type arrangements in Brazil and South Africa led to the formation of subsidiaries in each of those countries. In 1976 after lengthy negotiations, Richard Merwin founded EQUIMAG, or Equipmentos Magneticos do Brazil. In 1980 a new subsidiary, Eriez Magnetics South Africa, Ltd., began operating out of a Johannesburg suburb with Richard Merwin as Chairman.

By the time Richard Merwin assumed the chairmanship of the Board of Directors in 1986, he had already made Eriez' international sales and operations an integral part of the company. Overseas sales directly from Eriez or from its affiliates now account for over a third of the company's total sales volume and, occasionally, over half of its profits. For the future, Eriez is well-positioned to take advantage of growth opportunities in the Far East, Latin America, Southern Africa, and Europe. In addition, these far-flung operations provide the company with an invaluable window on new technology being developed around the world, some of it by its own affiliates. The work done by Eriez personnel on rare earth magnets and dry vibrating filters in Japan, on eddy-current separators in the United Kingdom, and on circular lifting magnets in Brazil are examples of the kind of innovations and improvements pioneered abroad that have helped keep Eriez in the forefront of technological advances.

International Division Personnel: *seated (left to right): Richard Merwin, Paul Hopsecger; standing: Kathy Heidt, Andrew Goldner, Rose McLaren.*

There are several reasons for the economic and technical success of Eriez' overseas affiliates. One of the most important is the company's ability to recruit and retain talented local management and staff, like Tadashi Homma in Japan, Fred Downie in the United Kingdom, Ron Poole in Australia, Mandi Lionello in South Africa, Edwin Rojas in Brazil, and Robert Gatt in Canada. Eriez strives to hire nationals who share the company's philosophy and who know their people and markets best. They have considerable autonomy in running their operations. Eriez treats its subsidiaries with respect and gives full recognition to their contributions. Following Bob Merwin's sage advice about the importance of admitting that we can learn from others, Eriez endeavors to ensure a two-way flow of ideas and experiences between headquarters and the affiliates that enriches both. Unlike many companies interested in foreign markets only on the basis of

ERIEZ OVERSEAS

← *Eriez Australia*

← *Eriez Canada*

← *Eriez Europe*

Eriez Mexico →

Eriez Japan →

Eriez South Africa →

getting in, grabbing quick profits and getting out as fast as possible, Eriez takes the long run view—it is there to stay and willing to reinvest a considerable portion of the profits to ensure a stable future.

If Eriez has been successful in pursuing its strategy of product, market and geographical diversity, one of the most important reasons for this success has been its evolution from a "basement technology" to an "advanced technology" company. Not long after O.F. Merwin and Marve Reynolds pieced together their first plate separator, Eriez began to recruit an outstanding team of engineers and technicians that over the years built the company's reputation as a true "pioneer" in processing equipment technology. From Ronnie Hoff and Arlo Israelson through Jim Torrey and Jim Floros to current Technical Director Richard Darling and Engineering Manager Jerry Rose, Eriez has always been blessed with the engineering talent and ingenuity needed to produce the steady stream of new and improved products upon which this reputation is based. The appointment of Dick Darling in 1990 to the newly-created position of Technical Director, Engineering and Research & Development was an important step towards the bolstering of that reputation. With a master's degree in Mechanical Engineering from Cornell University and nine years of service as Vice President of Engineering at W.S. Tyler Inc. of Gastonia, North Carolina, Darling possesses that combination of talent, vision and experience that have long been the hallmark of the company's top engineers.

Eriez' image as technological leader has been further bolstered by the many patents awarded its people and the even greater number of articles and papers, including a dozen written by Bob Merwin himself, produced for technical journals and conferences.

Anxious to retain its position as technological pacesetter in its field, Eriez has invested heavily in its Technical Center and the new CAD (Computer Aided Design) system for its technical staff. Realizing the importance of tapping the knowledge and experience of experts outside the company, the Board of Directors in 1981 created the Technical Advisory

Committee. TAC brought together
a select group of outside consultants
to meet with Eriez' own technical
people for regular meetings to discuss
new product development opportunities. Among the consultants who
served on TAC are Dr. Richard Smith
from the Argonne National Laboratory, Dr. Osman Mawardi, Professor
of Electrical Engineering at Case
Western University and President of
Collaborative Planners, Dr. Haydn
Murray, Chairman of the Geology
Department at Indiana University,
and Jerry Selvaggi, P.E., Associate

Jerry Selvaggi

Professor of Electrical Engineering at Gannon University.

No outside consultant has played a more prominent role in helping to
forge Eriez' enviable technological image than Jerry Selvaggi. He first
became associated with Eriez in 1968 when his assignment was to predict
mathematically how future products would perform so that testing would no
longer be a matter of "seeing what would happen" but of verifying the
predicted result. In addition to mathematical modeling, he also worked on
Eriez' unique computerized design program for use in product improvements. In recent years he led the Eriez team that developed the pathbreaking
Superconducting High Gradient Magnetic Separator.

Space does not permit a listing of the many "firsts" for which Eriez
products have become noted. Suffice it to say that in recent years the
company has continued to add to this list: the first in its field to use rare earth
magnets in its products; the first to develop the Superconducting HGMS;
the first to market an effective eddy-current separator; and the first to
develop the dry vibrating filter. These last three innovations deserve special

mention because they clearly demonstrate why Eriez' technological reputation is so well-deserved.

One of the most outstanding technical achievements in the company's history was the development of the Eriez Superconducting High Gradient Magnetic Separation System. In 1978 Eriez set out to design a practical cryogenic magnet system for commercial use. Within six years a task force headed by Jerry Selvaggi developed an operational prototype of 5-tesla (50,000 gauss) strength for laboratory research.

The first of three commercial superconducting systems was a 230 ton separator system to process kaolin clay at the J. M. Huber Co. of Wrens, Georgia. These units remove microsize impurities by the magnetic separation system.

Huber's Operations Manager, Joe Colwell, states: "Huber is benefitting from the stronger and more consistent 2-tesla field of the superconducting magnet. We have found that the operating economy is improved because we don't have to be concerned about the diminishing benefit-to-cost ratio of higher field strengths. The incremental cost of higher fields is negligible and we can, therefore, obtain greater kaolin brightness or higher throughput rates for small increases in operating expense."

Huber has found that fewer chemical additives are required with the new separator, which also takes up less space (34%) and weighs less (42%) than a conventional separator. EPA officials are now studying the environmental impact of this technology.

The superconducting system for Huber was the world's first successful use of a cryogenic magnet for industrial/commercial purposes. "Superconductivity may well be as close as science will ever come to energy-free separation," says Eriez president, Chet Giermak. "At the very least, cryogenics has brought about a whole new era of magnetic separation capabilities." The Huber application is blazing a trail for numerous other jobs such as waste-water treatment, coal purification, valuable mineral recovery, chemical processing, oil and ore refining, power generation, and in virtually any process where the removal of paramagnetic particles is critical.

Another of Eriez' exciting new products is the Second Generation Eddy Current Separator (ECS). It is a product whose time has come and it is proving to be one of the successful solutions to the problem of cleaning up the environment and recycling for profit.

In 1969 Eriez patented both permanent and electromagnetic Eddy Current Separators. The new second generation ECS features improved magnetic circuits using Rare Earth Magnets to produce stronger eddy currents and improved separation of non-ferrous materials.

The ECS can be used in a wide range of industrial materials recovery operations offering dependable and cost-effective separation of metallics from shredded municipal solid waste, shredded automobiles, plastics, rubber, glass, electronic scrap and other products.

Many products normally sent to landfills can now be effectively recycled. Some typical examples are:

- Removing up to 95% of the aluminum beverage cans from household trash
- Extracting metallics from mass burn boiler bottom ash
- Separating lead-bearing metallics from foundry sands
- Upgrading automobile shredder fluff
- Recycling spent pot linings from aluminum smelters
- Separating non-ferrous metallics like lead and aluminum from cullet

The Eriez ECS is making recycling possible, practical and profitable.

Another newly developed product, the Eriez Dry Vibrating Filter, was designed for applications where a high purity product is required in hard-to-handle powders. The separator consists of an open bore type electromagnet, a vibrating canister that houses a matrix (filter media) and a rectifier.

The electromagnet, when energized, induces a very strong magnetic field into the matrix which in turn amplifies the field and generates high gradient magnetic fields in the separating zone. While the non-magnetic product such as ceramic powders, pharmaceutical powders, finely ground industrial minerals, etc. filters through the separator, the magnetic impurities are effectively captured and retained in the matrix. The filter automatically discharges the contaminants with the assistance of an automated (programmable) cleaning system.

Eriez' continued ability to operate at the cutting edge of technology is

THE SECRETARY OF ENERGY
WASHINGTON, D.C. 20585

Greetings to Officers, Employees and Guests of Eriez
Magnetics at the Commissioning Ceremony for the Superconducting Magnetic Separation System:

For over 40 years, Eriez Magnetics has been recognized for its outstanding contributions to magnet technology. This facility, and the complex equipment that
it houses, represents an example of the kind of tools
that American scientists and engineers must have, if we
are to maintain our tradition of world leadership in
science and technology.

Your vision, and your willingness to invest in
the scientific enterprise, should serve as an inspira-
tion for other businesses whose future growth depends
upon innovation; and it should be seen as a vote of
confidence in the ability of your own staff, as they
seek to apply new scientific knowledge toward human
progress. To the extent you succeed in your purpose--
whether developing new materials recovery techniques,
achieving better energy efficiency technologies or
accomplishment in other areas--all Americans are potential beneficiaries.

I am honored to extend to you my personal best
wishes and congratulations.

Yours truly,

John S. Herrington

Letter sent to Eriez by Secretary of Energy John Herrington on the occasion of the commissioning of the company's laboratory model Superconducting High Gradient Magnetic Separator in 1985.

This 120-inch canister Superconducting High Gradient Magnetic Separator (HGMS) purifies kaolin clay which is used to make fine printing paper, ceramics, paints, adhesives, china, and other products.

The Eriez Eddy Current Separator.

testimony that the vision and pioneering spirit that marked the company's birth in 1942 are still present today. It is also clear that, as the company enters its second half-century, all those elements that brought Eriez to its position of world leadership remain in place: a strong Board of Directors; talented and experienced management; a customer-oriented sales, marketing and service organization; a problem-solving engineering and technical staff; and an office and production force that takes great pride in its work. Together this team of Eriez men and women produces a tremendous array of equipment for a host of diverse industries spread around the world. It is also constantly on the lookout for still more products, applications and markets.

As long as this team retains the pioneering spirit of Eriez' founders and remains faithful to the values they embodied in the company's Fundamental Principle, Eriez will continue to attract the wealth of talented, creative, motivated and loyal people who have made it what it is today—a world leader.

WORLD HEADQUARTERS

Eriez Manufacturing Company
Asbury Road at Airport
Erie, Pennsylvania
USA 16506
TEL: 814/833-9881
FAX: 814/838-4960

MANUFACTURING AFFILIATES

Eriez of Canada, Limited
Mississauga, Ontario
CANADA

Eriez Magnetics Japan Co., Limited
Tokyo
JAPAN

Eriez Magnetics Europe, Limited
Bedwas, Newport, Gwent
Wales
UNITED KINGDOM

Eriez Magnetics Pty., Limited
Campbellfield Victoria
AUSTRALIA

Eriez Equipos Magneticos, S.A. de C.V.
Mexico, 11550, D.F.
MEXICO

Eriez Magnetics (South Africa) (Pty.) Limited
Bramley, Transvaal
SOUTH AFRICA

Equimag
Sao Paulo
BRAZIL

APPENDIX

A   QUESTIONS AND ANSWERS REGARDING
    CHARACTERISTICS OF MAGNETS   102

B   Chart: HISTORY OF ENERGY PRODUCT FOR
    PERMANENT MAGNET MATERIALS   113

C   Table: RELATIVE ATTRACTABILITY OF MINERALS   114

D   Table: ERIUM PERMANENT MAGNETIC
    MATERIAL DATA   115

E   TECHNICAL BIBLIOGRAPHY   116

A
QUESTIONS AND ANSWERS
REGARDING CHARACTERISTICS OF MAGNETS

Engineers at Eriez are often asked about the characteristics of magnetism or magnetic devices. Some of the most frequently asked questions are presented below. The answers given are at a fairly basic technical level. For more detail the reader is referred to the Technical Bibliography which also appears in this Appendix.

Q. What is a magnet?   A. Webster defines a magnet as "Any body having the property of attracting iron." Soft iron may be converted temporarily into a magnet by contact with a magnet, by induction without contact, or by the influence of an electric current, in which case it is called an electromagnet.

Q. What is magnetism?   A. Textbooks usually describe magnetism by some of its attributes, such as its ability to attract iron, or to generate electricity when a conductor is passed through a magnetic field, as in a generator or magneto. Another definition: Magnetism is created by a flow of electricity in a conductor, as in an electromagnet or a motor.

We prefer to define magnetism as an external force due to electricity in motion, whether it be in a conductor or

from the uncompensated spins of elec-
trons in certain elements.

Q. Why is a piece of iron, or ferrous material, attracted to a magnet?

A. Iron is attracted to a magnet because a magnet induces opposite North and South poles in the iron. In other words, the iron becomes a temporary magnet and since opposite, or unlike, magnetic poles are attracted to each other, the iron is attracted to the magnet.

Q. Why is a small piece of iron attracted to the same magnet with less force than a larger piece?

A. The smaller piece of iron contains fewer magnetic force units (domains) so when both pieces are fully magnetized, the smaller piece becomes a smaller magnet than the larger. Both pieces are attracted to the parent magnet but in direct proportion to their own sizes. The amount of attraction is also influenced by the gradient and flux density of the magnetic field.

Q. What is magnetic flux?

A. Magnetic flux is a technical name for the magnetic field. More specifically, the magnetic flux is that condition produced in a given region by a magnet, such that when that condition is altered in magnitude, an electric current is produced in a circuit surrounding the given region.

Q. How is magnetic flux characterized?

A. The unit of measure of the magnetic field or flux density is the Gauss. The magnetic flux density is measured with instruments which indicate the number of imaginary lines of flux passing through a square centimeter of area oriented perpendicular to the direction of the magnetic field. When discussing the strength characteristics of a magnet, we may say it has a flux density of "2000 Gauss"; meaning, 2000 lines per square centimeter.

Q. What other factors determines the attraction exerted by a magnet?

A. The attraction of a magnet is determined by both the magnetic field and the change in magnetic field (flux gradient) between points measured at different distances perpendicular to the magnetic field. The greater the change in flux density, the greater the magnetic attraction...especially when we are concerned with the magnetic attraction of small particles. A uniform magnetic field, with no gradient, would have no attractive force in a direction parallel with the uniformity. In two fields of the same flux density the one with a high gradient will attract ferrous materials with a greater force. This is because of the field pattern induced in the attracted particle.

Q. **What elements are classified as magnetic, or have significant magnetic characteristics?**

A. The most important elements at this time are iron, nickel, cobalt and some of the rare earth elements.

Q. **How does a piece of magnetic material become magnetized?**

A. A material is said to be magnetized when it is exposed to a magnetic field strong enough to cause orientation or alignment of the magnetic force elements (domains) that are present in all magnetic materials. When removed from a magnetic field iron usually loses its magnetism; the magnetism induced in a permanent magnet remains indefinitely unless exposed to strong demagnetizing influences. The magnetism remaining in a material after its removal from the magnetizing force is known as the residual magnetism. When the material is completely magnetized, or oriented, and cannot produce any greater reponse if exposed to a stronger magnetic field, it is said to be saturated.

The ratio of magnetization to the magnetic force applied is called the susceptibility of the material.

Q. **How are magnetic materials classified?**

A. If the atoms of a material have a magnetic moment even when no external field is present, a bar of that material will tend to align itself with any external magnetic field that is applied. Such a material is termed _paramagnetic_, or in the extreme case, _ferromagnetic_. When the atoms of a material do not normally have a magnetic moment in the absence of an external magnetic field, the material is classified as _diamagnetic_. When a bar of diamagnetic material is exposed to a powerful external magnetic field, there will be a slight field induced in the material, but the field will have the same polarity as the external field, and the bar will align itself perpendicular to the applied field.

Q. **Why do minerals have such a wide range of magnetic susceptibility?**

A. In order to be attracted to a magnet any mineral must contain some of the magnetic elements. The various minerals have different amounts and combinations of these elements, hence they can be categorized as _strongly magnetic, moderately magnetic, weakly magnetic and feebly magnetic_. Of course, minerals with no magnetic elements are non-magnetic.

Q. **Why is iron sometimes non-magnetic, or paramagnetic?**

A. Iron may become non-magnetic by absorbing non-magnetic elements, such as oxygen, which change the internal structure necessary for magnetism. The oxides in mill scale and in some iron ores are examples of this.

Q. **Can other materials, such as copper or aluminum, be magnetized if exposed to very strong magnetic fields?**

A. No, they cannot become permanent magnets. However, a transient magnetic field can be induced in conductors by the eddy currents generated by an alternating nearby magnetic field.

Q. **Is there any insulator for a magnetic field?**

A. There is no known insulator for a magnetic field. However, the field can be baffled by a like magnetic field or can be shielded by steel or iron.

Q. **What is magnetic permeability?**

A. The term "magnetic permeability" describes magnetic materials as to their relative abilities to conduct magnetism. Numerically, permeability is the ratio of the flux density to the magnetizing force in a given material.

Q. **What is the inverse square law?**

A. This law of physics states that the strength of a magnet varies inversely as the square of the distance from the magnet. It is because of this law that the field of even the strongest magnet is extremely limited in depth. A strong magnet might be capable of holding a ton of steel on its surface, yet be incapable of lifting a paper clip at a distance of thirty-six inches.

Q. What is a permanent magnet?

A. In addition to the geometry and strength of the magnet itself, the shape of a magnetic field is determined by the air gap and the pole plates. The air gap is the external space between the North and South poles of any magnet. The pole plates are usually iron or steel pieces attached to the North and South poles of magnets which by their shapes and spacing can, within limits, control the configuration and gradient of the magnetic field. They also permit combining groups of magnets into single magnets.

Q. What determines the shape of a magnetic field?

A. A permanent magnet is a body which, after being magnetized, can retain the induced magnetism indefinitely. All permanent magnets have North and South poles. A permanent magnet can be broken into any number of smaller pieces but each piece will still have its own North and South poles.

Q. What is an electromagnet?

A. An electromagnet is a magnet created by passing a flow of direct current electricity through a coil or conductor which surrounds an iron core. The flow of electricity aligns the magnetic forces inherent in the iron causing the iron to become a magnet with North and South poles...while the electric current is flowing. When the current flow is stopped the iron core returns to its normal state and ceases to be a magnet. When magnetic fields of permanent and electromagnets are of the same size and configuration their effect on magnetic materials is identical.

Q. What are the major differences between the three commonly used permanent magnet materials: Alnico, Ferrite, and Rare Earth magnets?

A. Alnico magnets are cast alloys of iron, nickel, cobalt and other elements that are very strong magnetically, usually requiring less space than ferrite magnets to produce the same magnetic strength. Pound for pound they are generally more expensive than Ferrite. They can tolerate broad temperature ranges.

Ferrite magnets are usually pressings of strontium ferric oxide. They may also consist of this material embedded in a rubber or polymer matrix. If they are properly designed they can often equal or exceed the strength of Alnico magnets at less cost. However, they are subject to a greater variation in strength when exposed to variations in temperature. They have replaced Alnico in most applications.

There are two types of Rare Earth magnets. The first is a sintered alloy of rare earth and cobalt. The rare earth material is typically samarium, but is not limited to that element. These magnets are much stronger than either Ferrite or Alnico, but at a much higher cost. The second type is either a sintered or melt spun alloy of neodymium, iron and boron. These magnets are the strongest of all present day commercial magnets. While they cost less than samarium cobalt magnets they are limited to a narrower temperature range.

All Rare Earth magnets are extremely resistant to demagnetizing influences.

Q. What are demagnetizing influences?

A. For Alnico there are three major demagnetizing influences.
1. Forcing like poles together repeatedly.
2. Disassembly of assemblies that have been magnetized as a unit.
3. Allowing iron or other magnetic materials to contact magnet castings in areas other than on the working faces.

For ferrite and rare earth magnets we are not usually concerned with demagnetizing influences except for extreme temperatures.

Q. **What are typical temperature limits for Alnico, Ferrite, and Rare Earth magnets?**

A. For Alnico there is no lower limit on temperature. At the high end, Alnico magnets can operate safely in temperatures of 750°F to 800°F. Alnico magnets will experience approximately a 1% reversible loss in field strength for each 100°F temperature elevation above room temperature.

Ferrite magnet strength generally falls about 10% below maximum for each 100°F elevation above room temperature. A ferrite magnet will generally regain its strength upon return to room temperature. However, if exposed to temperatures above 850°F, a ferrite magnet will demagnetize and must be remagnetized. At lower temperatures (with proper design) most ferrite magnet assemblies can safely withstand −40°F without requiring remagnetization.

Rare Earth magnets will experience a reversible loss of their magnetic field of about 2.5% and 5.5% for each 100°F elevation above room temperature for samarium cobalt and neodymium-iron-boron respectively. While a properly designed samarium cobalt magnet is not restricted by a low temperature limit, the neodymium-iron-boron magnet is limited to about −100°F no matter what design is used. The maximum operating temperature for the Rare Earth magnets is 570°F for samarium cobalt, and 300°F for neodymium-iron-boron. Various compositions can, however, modify the temperature limit at the expense of some other property.

Q. Is physical shock harmful to the magnetism of permanent magnets?

A. No. This belief is a carryover from many years ago when the first permanent magnets were vulnerable to shock or vibration. In fact, permanent magnets are now used in impact type vibratory products, where continued shock is severe, without harm to the magnets.

Q. How long will a permanent magnet retain its strength?

A. Unless it is exposed to the demagnetizing influences previously mentioned, a permanent magnet should retain its strength indefinitely. However, we generally say that the strength will diminish at 0.1% to 0.5% per century.

Q. Will using a magnet accelerate its loss of strength?

A. The answer to this is a definite "No", unless the magnet is misused or abused.

B
HISTORY OF ENERGY PRODUCT
FOR PERMANENT MAGNET MATERIALS

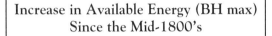

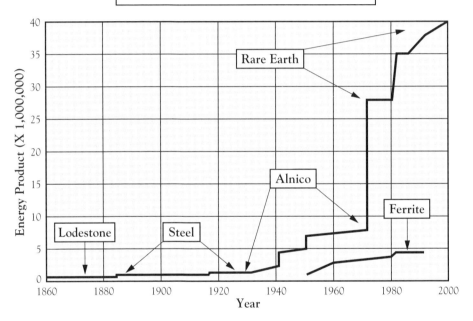

C
RELATIVE ATTRACTABILITY OF MINERALS

MINERAL	SOURCE OF SAMPLE	RA*	MINERAL	SOURCE OF SAMPLE	RA*
Group 1 - Ferromagnetic (Approximately 500-5,000 gauss required for separation)					
Iron		100.000	Magnetite	Port Henry, NY	14.862
Magnetite	Unknown	48.000	Franklinite	Franklin Furnace, NJ	13.089
Group 2 - Moderately Magnetic (Approximately 5,000-10,000 gauss required for separation)					
Ilmenite	Edge Hill, PA	9.139	Franklinite	Franklin Furnace, NJ	1.480
Pyrrhotite	Sudbury, ONT	2.490			
Group 3 - Weakly Magnetic (Approximately 10,000-18,000 gauss required for separation)					
Hematite	Lake Superior district	0.769	Bornite	New South Wales, Australia	0.086
Siderite	Roxbury, CT	0.743	Apatite	Eganville, Ontario	0.083
Rhodonite	Franklin Furnace, NJ	0.560	Tetrahedrite	Peru	0.080
Limonite	Nova Scotia	0.314	Willemite	Franklin Furnace, NJ	0.076
Braunite	Italy	0.300	Bornite	Union Bridge, MD	0.067
Corundum	Gaston County, NC	0.264	Sphalerite	Iowa	0.057
Hematite	Cumberland, England	0.257	Cerrusite	New South Wasle, Australia	0.057
Pyrolusite	Bartow County, GA	0.248	Dolomite	Sing Sing, NY	0.057
Manganite	Bridgeville, Nova Scotia	0.194	Psilomelane	North Mt. Mine, AR	0.056
Calamine	Friedensville, PA	0.187	Arsenopyrite	Acton, York Co., ME	0.054
Sphalerite	Frieburg, Germany	0.182	Sphene (Titanite)	Murchison Township, Ontario	0.054
Siderite	Unknown	0.160	Chalcopyrite	South Australia	0.051
Rhodochrosite	Argentina	0.152	Molybdenite	New South Wales, Australia	0.048
Garnet	Unknown	0.149	Talc	Swain Co., NC	0.042
Serpentine, green	Unknown	0.140	Celesite	Strontium Island, OH	0.038
Molybdenite	Frankford, PA	0.118	Chalcocite	Butte, MT	0.038
Mica, spotted	Bengal, India	0.115	Cinnabar	New Almaden, CA	0.038
Corundum	Lehigh County, PA	0.111	Gypsum	Derbyshire, England	0.038
Cerargyrite	New Mexico	0.105	Zincite	Franklin Furnace, NJ	0.038
Huebnerite	Henderson, NC	0.105	Orthoclase	Elam, PA	0.035
Wolframite	Chochiwon, Kenya	0.105	Epidote	Unknown	0.033
Argentite	Guanajuato, Mexico	0.102	Flourite	Rosiclare, IL	0.032
Ferberite	Malaya	0.101	Augite	Unknown	0.027
Wolframite	Climax, CO	0.100	Hornblende	Unknown	0.025
Group 4 - Feebly Magnetic (over 18,000 gauss required for separation)					
Pyrite	Rio Tinto, Spain	0.022	Chrysocolla	Miami, AZ	0.0063
Smithsonite	Kelly, NM	0.022	Rutile	Unknown	0.0034
Sphalerite	Joplin, MO	0.022	Mica, ruby, clear	Bengal, India	0.0032
Stibnite	Germany	0.022	Orthoclase	Alexandria, NY	0.0032
Cryolite	Greenland	0.019	Limestone	Unknown	0.0024
Enargite	Butte, MT	0.019	Cobalite	Unknown	0.0023
Senarmonite	Unknown	0.019	Sapphire	Unknown	0.0023
Magnesite	Lancaster Co., TX	0.019	Pyrite	Unknown	0.002
Azurite	Chessy, France	0.018	Cassiterite	Cornwall, England	0.0019
Gysum	Grand Rapids, MI	0.016	Tourmaline	Unknown	0.0012
Malachite	Katanga, Africa	0.016	Dolomite	Unknown	0.0011
Niccolite	Bebra Hesse, Germany	0.016	Spinel	Unknown	0.0010
Serpentine, red	Unknown	0.016	Beryl	Unknown	0.0008
Stibnite	Juab Co., UT	0.013	Ruby	Unknown	0.0008
Dioptase	Unknown	0.012	Covellite	Butte, MT	0.0007
Tourmaline	Unknown	0.0012	Fledspar	Unknown	0.0006
Cuprite	Cornwall, England	0.0096	Sphalerite	Jeferson City, TN	0.0005
Galena	Galena, IL	0.0096	Zircon	Unknown	0.0002
Witherite	Cumberland, England	0.0064			
Group 5 - Nonmagnetic and Diamagnetic					
Barite	Bartow Co., GA	0.0	Corundum	Unknown	-0.0006
Adularia	Unknown	-0.0004	Topaz	Unknown	-0.0006
Calcite	Unknown	-0.0004	Galena	Unknown	-0.0011
Flourite	Unknown	-0.0004	Antimony, native	Unknown	-0.0023
Halite	Unknown	-0.0004	Bismuth	Unknown	-0.0032
Sphalerite	Unknown	-0.0004	Apatite	Unknown	-0.0034
Celestite	Unknown	-0.0005	Argonite	Unknown	-0.0048
Quartz	Unknown	-0.0005	Graphite	Ceylon	-0.032

*NOTES: RA = Relative Attractability. Relative attractability will vary according to source of sample. Relative attractabilities for this chart were calculated using the volume susceptibility of 250,000 x 10^{-6} as equal to 100.

D
ERIUM PERMANENT MAGNETIC MATERIAL DATA

NAME (Type)	ERIUM 45 (Alnico)	ERIUM 25 (Ferrite Ceramic)	ERIUM 12 (Ferrite Rubber)	ERIUM 3000 (Rare Earth)
Manufacturing Process	Foundry casting or sintered, using pattern or shell molding, cooled in oriented field.	Wet or dry powders pressed under high pressures. Fired in high temperature ovens.	Calendar rolls using rubber processing methods. Also extrusions.	Powder metallurgy, sinter, heat treat.
Composition	8% Al, 14% Ni, 24% Co, 3% Cu, Bal Fe.	$MO 6 Fe_2O_3$	Approx 11% rubber and 89% strontium ferrite by wt.	30% Nd, 2% B, balance Fe.
Density #/cu. in.	0.265	0.176	0.134	0.27
Practical Maximum Energy Product (Million Gauss-Oersteds)	Unoriented Al II, III: 2.4 Oriented Al V: 5.5 Directional grain Al V: 7.5	Oriented: 3.25-3.5 Unoriented (Erium 21): 1.0	Oriented: 1.0 Unoriented (Erium 10): 0.4	35.0
Temperature Limitations	No cold effects. 10% loss to 750°F. Recommended operating temp 930°F or less.	Design determines cold temperature limits. 10% reversible loss for each 100°F increase above room temperature.	Same as strontium ferrite with rubber limitations -- about 200°F.	302°F.
Size Limitations	"C" or straight castings.	1" thick pressings, 8" square.	1/2" thick rubber sheets.	1/2" thick sections.
Curie Point	1,634°F.	842°F.	Rubber limitations.	590°F.
Physical Data	Hard, semi brittle (special abrasive wheels required to cut). Not practical to drill holes.	Hard, brittle (diamond cutters required).	Similar to hard, brittle rubber. Abrasive knives required to cut to size.	Hard, semi-brittle, difficult to machine.
Hardness	50 R/C		65 durometer "D".	58 R/C.
Shapes Available	Horseshoe, straight, and ring shapes.	Flat (1" thk max) pressings. Oriented material has poles on pressed sides.	Flat sheets and extruded lengths.	Flat rectangles, rings, arc sections.
Shrinkage in Process	Nil	17%	Nil	13%
Weight Comparison / Equal Energy	1.0#	1.25# to 1.5#	Approximately 3.0#	0.16#
Volume Comparison / Equal Energy	1.0in³.	1.83in³.	Approximately 6.0in³.	0.15in³.
Tooling	Foundry type patterns, cost $100 to $500.	Expensive carbide tooling dies, $100 to $5000 each.	Rubber processing equipment.	Tooling dies or isostatic pressing.
Electrical Resistivity Micro-Ohms per cm/cm2	47	10^{10}	10^{12}	150
Corrosion	Little or none under almost all conditions.	None.	Limited to rubber characteristics.	Nd oxide forms on surface.
Largest Available Sizes	Practical size is about 25# maximum.	1" thick about 8" square. Laminate pieces for larger volumes.	1/2" thick x 24" square, also long extruded lengths.	4" dia x 10" long isostatic, 3" square x 5/8" thick die press.
Tolerances	Approx 1/16" on cast surfaces. Grinding tolerances on finished surfaces.	+ 1/8" outside surfaces. + .085" pressed surfaces. Grinding tolerances on finished surfaces.	Rubber limitations.	Approx 1/16" on pressing surf, grind other surfaces.
Fastening Means	Slots, cored holes.	Cements, slots, physical clamps.Cements, clamps.	Cements, clamps.	Cements, physical clamps.
Magnetic Force	3,000 oersteds	10,000 oersteds	10,000 oersteds	30,000-50,000 oersteds
Relative Magnet Areas Required	1.0in².	4.0 to 5.0in².	10.0in².	1.56in².
Relative Magnet Lengths Required	3.5 inches	1.0 inch	1.0 inch	0.55 inches
Residual Flux Density (Gauss) Coercive Force (oersteds)	12,500 685	3,850-4,200 2,400	2,360 1,960	12,300 11,300

E
TECHNICAL BIBLIOGRAPHY

Bozorth, R.M., <u>Ferromagnetism</u>, New York: D. Van Nostrand Co., Inc., 1951

Brechna, H., <u>Superconducting Magnet Systems</u>, New York: Springer-Verlag, 1973

Brechna, H. and Gordon H.S., <u>Proceeding of the International Symposium on Magnet Technology</u>, Virginia: F.S.T.I./ N.B.S. U.S. Dept. of Commerce, 1965

Burke, Harry E., <u>Handbook of Magnetic Phenomena</u>, New York: Van Nostrand Reinhold Co., 1986

Kolm, H., Lax B., Bitter F. Mills R., <u>High Magnetic Fields</u>, New York: John Wiley & Sons Inc., 1961

Kroon, D.J., <u>Electromagnets</u>, Mass.: Boston Technical Publishers, 1968.

McCaig, Malcolm, <u>Permanent Magnets in Theory and Practice</u>, New York: Halsted Press, 1977.

Mitchell, I.V., <u>Nd-Fe Permanent Magnets Their Present and Future Applications</u>, New York: Elsevier Applied Science Pub., 1985.

Montgomery, B.D., <u>Solenoid Market Design</u>, New York: Robert E. Krieger Pub. Co., 1980.

Moskowitz, Lester R., <u>Permanent Magnet Design and Application Handbook</u>, Mass.: Cahners Books Int. Inc., 1976.
Nesbitt, E.A. and Wernick, J.H., <u>Rare Earth Permanent Magnets</u>, New York: Academic Press, 1973.

Parker, Rollin J., <u>Advances in Permanent Magnetism</u>, New York: Wiley-Interscience, 1990.

Parker, Rollin J. and Studders, Robert J., <u>Permanent Magnets and Their Application</u>, New York: John Wiley and Sons, Inc., 1962.

Phillips, J.C., <u>Physics of High-T_c Superconductors</u>, New York: Academic Press, Inc., 1989.

Rotors, H.C., <u>Electromagnetic Devices</u>, New York: John Wiley & Sons Inc., 1941.

Smith, Steve, <u>Magnetic Components Design and Application</u>, New York: Van Nostrand Reinhold Co., 1985.

Stratton, J.A., <u>Electromagnetic Theory</u>, New York: McGraw Hill Book Co., 1941.

Wilson, Martin N., <u>Superconducting Magnets</u>, New York: Oxford Science Publications, 1983.

Wohlfarth, E.P. and Buschow, K.H.J., <u>Ferro-Magnetic Materials</u>, New York: North-Holland, 1988.